Designing
Engineering
Solutions

Inventors of Communications Technology

Heather S. Morrison

Cavendish
Square
New York

CPSIA Compliance Information: Batch #WS15CSQ

All websites were available and accurate when this book was sent to press.

Library of Congress Cataloging-in-Publication Data

Morrison, Heather S.
Inventors of communications technology / Heather S. Morrison.
pages cm. — (Designing engineering solutions)
Includes bibliographical references and index.
ISBN 978-1-50260-656-3 (hardcover) ISBN 978-1-50260-657-0 (ebook)
1. Inventors—Juvenile literature. 2. Communication and technology—Juvenile literature. I. Title.

T48.M73 2016
621.382092'2—dc23

2014049219

The author would like to thank the following contributors: Laura Lambert, Mary Sisson, Cathleen Small, Chris Woodford

Editorial Director: David McNamara
Editor: Kristen Susienka
Copy Editor: Rebecca Rohan
Art Director: Jeffrey Talbot
Designer: Alan Sliwinski
Senior Production Manager: Jennifer Ryder-Talbot
Production Editor: Renni Johnson
Photo Research: J8 Media

The photographs in this book are used by permission and through the courtesy of: Winhorse/E+/Getty Images, cover; Public Domain/File:Treatise of the World's Creation WDL10602.pdf/Wikimedia Commons, 4; Look and Learn/ Illustrated Papers Collection/Bridgeman Art Library, 7; Rock and Wasp/Shutterstock.com, 15; SSPL/Getty Images, 17; Public Domain/File:Photo of Alexander Graham Bell.jpg/Wikimedia Commons, 18; Private Collection/Bridgeman Art Library, 22; Blackboard1965/Shutterstock.com, 27; Photos.com/Thinkstock, 28; Bill Greene/The Boston Globe/Getty Images, 32; Alsu/Shutterstock.com, 35; Apic/Hulton Archive/Getty Images, 36; PHAS/UIG/Getty Images, 39; Yorick Jansens/AFP/Getty Images, 42; Tomasz Sienicki/File:An mp3-player (ubt 147).jpg/Wikimedia Commons, 45; Rico Shen/ File:2007Computex e21Forum-MartinCooper.jpg/Wikimedia Commons, 46; Public Domain/File:Skype-icon.png/ Wikimedia Commons, 49; Matthew Staver/Bloomberg/Getty Images (left), Brian Ach/Getty Images for TechCrunch (right), 50; Rocketclips, Inc./Shutterstock.com, 55; SSPL/Getty Images, 58; Courtesy AMPEX, 59; Marc Bryan-Brown/ WireImage/Getty Images, 61; Skylines/Shutterstock.com, 65; Public Domain/File:Johannes Gutenberg.jpg/Wikimedia Commons, 66; Authenticated News/Getty Images, 69; Asharkyu/Shutterstock.com, 74; Michael Rougier/The LIFE Picture Collection/Getty Images, 75; Gilo1969/File:Gastroscope.jpg/Wikimedia Commons, 79; Steveball/Shutterstock.com, 82; Thomas D. Mcavoy/The LIFE Picture Collection/Getty Images, 83; Public Domain/MGM/File:Hedy Lamarr-1942.jpg/ Wikimedia Commons, 84; Victorgrigas/File:Institut Lumière - CINEMATOGRAPHE Camera.jpg/Wikimedia Commons, 88; SSPL/Getty Images, 89; HABRDA/Shutterstock.com, 96; SSPL/Getty Images, 98; File:Guglielmo Marconi posing. jpg/Wikimedia Commons, 99; Keystone-France/Gamma - Keystone/Getty Images, 105; Public Domain/Evan-Amos/ File:Sony-wm-fx421-walkman.jpg/Wikimedia Commons, 107; AFP/Getty Images, 108; Charnsitr/Shutterstock.com, 113; Underwood Archives/Archive Photos/Getty Images, 115; Hulton Archive/Getty Images, 116; Old Visuals/Age Fotostock, 119; Public Domain/George Iles/File:Sholes typewriter.jpg/Wikimedia Commons, 124; NYPL/Science Source/Getty Images, 125; Public Domain/File:TypewriterPatent1868.jpg/Wikimedia Commons, 129.

Printed in the United States of America

Contents

Introduction to Communications Technology

Technology is a means to help humans record and store information, and to connect with other people. Since the first technological advances, many other forms of technology have evolved. One area is communications technology. Being able to communicate with each other is essential to our society. Devices such as cell phones, word processors, televisions, and radios help others communicate on a more personal level. These advances have changed the way people interact with each other and have propelled our society into a more technologically able and dependent body. However, technology took time to develop. Many people played roles in advancing the technology industry to where it is today.

Humans are social beings, so the problem of how to share information more effectively has always taxed inventors. A few thousand years ago, communication meant storing ideas and relating them to people in the immediate vicinity, using inventions such as the alphabet and written language. In the early twenty-first century, global communication is just as important and is facilitated by fiber **optics** and the Internet. Inventors and thinkers did not simply use science to move from the alphabet to the discoveries and technologies that permitted the development of the Internet; they both drove and were driven by wider changes in society.

Evolution of Communications Technology

The earliest forms of writing were records of trade, kept in the Middle East around ten thousand years ago and consisting of clay tablets or bone. Around six thousand years later (circa 1700 BCE), the Semites of the Mediterranean devised an alphabet. Dozens of inventions have since improved the way people store and share written language.

The first books were religious ones. An early book was not printed, like the books of today, but laboriously copied by hand onto a wax tablet called a **codex**. Later books were copied into large volumes made from parchment and **vellum** (durable writing materials produced from animal skins) bound in leather. In 105 CE a Chinese court official named Cai Lun (also known as Ts'ai Lun) invented paper based on tree bark, which was lighter, easier to produce, and less expensive. This enabled the Chinese to develop printing about four hundred years later. They laboriously carved an entire page of text into a large wooden block, covered it with ink, and pressed it onto the paper.

Another key advance took place around 1450 CE when a German named Johannes Gutenberg (ca. 1400–1468) invented printing with movable type. Instead of using one large **printing block** per page, Gutenberg used many tiny blocks, each capable of printing one letter, and he moved them around in a special frame, or form, so these separate blocks could be used again and again to print different words. Few people were literate in Europe in the Middle Ages, so most of the books printed on Gutenberg's press were religious works;

priests and other officials of the Christian church were often literate and educated. The Bible was the first book Gutenberg printed, and around fifty copies of his version survive today. Once invented, Gutenberg's printing technology spread rapidly, carrying religious, political, and scientific information with it. By 1500, an estimated forty thousand books were in print in fourteen European countries.

During the Industrial Revolution of the nineteenth century, the speed and volume of **commerce** increased, and old-fashioned handwriting, using pens dipped into inkwells, could no longer keep up. The nineteenth century brought new writing and printing technologies, including the steel-nibbed pen (1803), the graphite pencil (1812), and raised-dot writing for the blind, invented in the 1820s by Louis Braille (1809–1852). Lewis Waterman (1837–1901), an insurance clerk, invented the fountain pen, which carried its own ink supply, in 1884. He wanted people to be able to sign his contracts more quickly. The even more convenient ballpoint pen, which applied thicker, quick-drying ink to paper using a tiny rolling ball, appeared in 1938, thanks to Hungarian Laszlo Biro (1899–1985).

The typewriter, developed by Christopher Latham Sholes (1819–1890) in 1868, was an even more far-reaching invention; it put the power of Gutenberg's movable-type printing press into the hands of individuals. With a typewriter, anyone could produce professional-looking printed materials. Quick and simple copying of documents, however, was not possible until 1938, when Chester Carlson (1906–1968) invented the photocopier.

Writing and printing technology allowed people to store and share their thoughts more easily and to pass on ideas to those who followed. The development of information-storing technologies, from written language to the photocopier, partly explains why the pace of invention is quicker now than it was thousands of years ago.

Transporting Messages and Sounds

Initial improvements in communication came about largely through improvements in transportation. Over the centuries, messages were relayed across long distances by everything from marathon runners

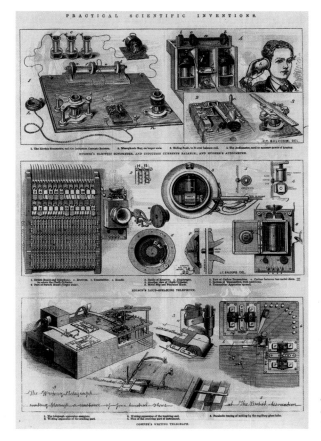

An illustration featuring different "practical scientific inventions" from 1879

and carrier pigeons in ancient Greece to stagecoaches, the Pony Express, and railroad locomotives in nineteenth-century America.

All this changed with the growing scientific understanding of electricity and the realization that it could be harnessed for practical purposes. One of the most important discoveries was that electricity and magnetism were part of the same underlying phenomenon, **electromagnetism**, and either of them could cause the other. By 1837, English physicists Charles Wheatstone (1802–1875) and William Cooke (1806–1879) had sent simple electric messages down a cable, using magnetic compass needles to signal when the message arrived at the other end. This early electric telegraph was quickly superseded by a better system that artist Samuel Morse (1791–1872) developed in the United States in the 1840s. Like the transcontinental railroads that were laid across North America in the nineteenth century, the telegraph played a vital role in the westward expansion of the United States by helping the government to communicate rapidly with its new territories and control them effectively. By the end of the nineteenth century, the telegraph had spread worldwide, with countries linked by cables laid beneath the oceans. Communications technology was beginning to knit the world together.

"You see, wire telegraph is a kind of very, very long cat. You pull his tail in New York and his head is meowing in Los Angeles. Do you understand this? And radio operates in exactly the same way: you send signals here, they receive them there. The only difference is that there is no cat."

—Albert Einstein

Signaling systems, including the electric telegraph, were similar to printing inasmuch as they were forms of communication that individuals could not readily use themselves—they were too costly or cumbersome or they required special equipment and skilled operators. If a person wanted a pamphlet printed, it would have to be "set" in type and published by a skilled printer who owned a printing press. In the same way, if a person wanted to send a message from New York to Washington, DC, a telegraph operator with the right equipment and trained in Morse code had to send it for that person.

Just as the typewriter and photocopier put powerful printing technology in the hands of individuals, the telephone, **patented** in 1876 by Alexander Graham Bell (1847–1922), accomplished the same end for long-distance communications.

By the dawn of the twenty-first century, many of the world's original copper telephone wires had been replaced by fiber-optic cables, which carry huge amounts of voice, fax, and Internet data as tiny pulses of laser light. Indian physicist Narinder Kapany (1927–) invented these remarkable "light pipes" in 1954 while he was studying in London. The fiber-optic revolution is an example of how social needs and technological developments constantly drive each other forward; high-capacity fiber-optic cables have made possible faster, cheaper international telephone calls and underpinned the growth of the global Internet. The demand for these services has been so great that scientists have been spurred on to develop even higher-capacity fiber-optic technologies.

Use of the telephone spread rapidly because it required no special skills, although for many decades trained operators were needed, first to connect all calls and later to handle long-distance and international calls. By the end of the twentieth century, almost all calls could be made directly by individuals, who had only to pick up a handset and dial the correct series of numbers. Communication became more immediate, more direct, and less formal. Unlike every previous form of long-distance communication, the telephone bypassed the need for written language and carried people's immediate thoughts, as well as their words, across geographic divides. When the telephone was first invented, the telegraph still had one major advantage: it could be connected to a hole-punching device that would automatically record incoming messages onto a reel of ticker tape that could be read later. The telegraph printer, with its famous ticker tape, revolutionized stock trading. It gave buyers and sellers the advantage of getting financial information more quickly and easily, greatly increased the volume of stock trading, and ultimately made Wall Street the major financial center in the United States.

The inventor of ticker tape, the prolific inventor Thomas Edison (1847–1931), quickly realized that something similar was needed for the telephone. In 1877, he invented the world's first telephone-answering machine—a rotating foil cylinder into which a vibrating needle dug grooves. German engineer Emile Berliner (1851–1929) realized the entertainment potential of this "talking machine," turned Edison's device into the gramophone, and launched the world's first record label (Victor) to market recordings for it. By 1948, gramophone records had become long-playing records (LPs) capable of storing roughly an hour of sound on two sides of a plastic disk. With the arrival of recorded music, singers and musicians became as important as the composers of music—their recordings, which would still be available after their deaths, potentially secured their fame.

LPs evolved into compact discs during the late 1960s because of research by US physicist James Russell (1931–).

Gramophones put prerecorded sound into the hands of ordinary people. The technology that allowed people to actually record sound was pioneered by another American inventor, Oberlin Smith (1840–1926). Building on Edison's work, Smith invented ways of recording sounds on cloth coated with magnetic chemicals. The German AEG Company commercialized this idea in 1935; its magnetophone could store sound by magnetizing a plastic tape covered with iron oxide that was wrapped into long reels. In the early 1950s, the American

Developing Communications Technology

Imagine what communications technology would have been like in the nineteenth century. Most people lived near their immediate family and friends, so people would have had little need to send messages long distances; they spoke to one another in person or carried information on foot or horseback instead. For reaching more distant contacts, such as family members who had migrated to become pioneer settlers in the West, there was always the mail. The US Post Office was created in 1789 and, although originally the country had only seventy-five post offices, the service rapidly expanded, following rivers and—much later—railroads into the new territories. Initially, mail took more than a month to travel from Washington, DC, to Nebraska by stagecoach. American Express, which was originally a stagecoach company, was founded in 1850; Wells Fargo followed in 1852.

Sending mail between Missouri and California was slightly quicker if the correspondents used the Pony Express, established in 1860. This glamorous mail service advertised for "young, skinny, wiry fellows, not over eighteen, expert riders, willing to risk death daily, orphans preferred" to carry small packets in the saddlebags of swift horses. Pony Express was the email of its day but was rendered obsolete after only eighteen months by the arrival of the telegraph.

The great transportation and communications developments of the nineteenth century—railroads, the telegraph, and the electrical engineer Charles Ginsburg (1920–1992) used similar technology to store television pictures, thus inventing the videotape recorder. During the 1960s, engineers at the Dutch company Royal Philips Electronics squeezed huge reels of magnetic tape into tiny, convenient "compact cassettes" that could hold up to two hours of audio. Cassettes made recording sound easy, and when Akio Morita (1921–1999) invented the Sony Walkman in the 1980s, people could play music wherever they went. Compact audiocassettes revolutionized the way people listened to music, and a similar transformation turned Charles Ginsburg's cumbersome videotape reels into videocassettes, which also became popular in the 1980s.

telephone—allowed people to keep in touch even as they traveled ever farther. These remarkable inventions allowed societies to reach outward and created, in their turn, the need for even better forms of communication. They also allowed national and eventually global markets to expand so greatly that people no longer think much about where goods and produce originate or how they reach their markets (in the early nineteenth century, almost all business and commerce was local).

In the twenty-first century, with television pictures flooding in from around the world, people take global communications for granted. They can send text messages via their smartphones or instant messages over the Internet to friends on the other side of the world and get replies in seconds. In the nineteenth century, before telegraph and telephone cables were laid in the oceans, communicating with those in other countries could be done only by sending letters on ships, which could take months. A year or more could pass before a reply to a letter was received.

In only a matter of centuries, technology has advanced to become truly a modern marvel. One wonders what the future of technology holds and what other previously slower mechanisms of communication will take off to become something instantly accessible. Only time will tell.

Inventions That Moved the World

Telegraphs and telephones connected the world by wires from the middle of the nineteenth century onward, but their big drawback was that they allowed communication only between fixed points. Nowhere was this problem more acute than on ships, one of the most important military technologies of the time. As business and commerce entered the telecommunications age, the battleships that waged wars and conquered nations seemed stuck behind in an earlier epoch. To send messages between one another and to the shore, they used primitive and unreliable methods like flashing lights and semaphore flags—useless over long distances and in bad weather.

Radio revolutionized shipping, especially in military operations. The young Italian who developed radio, Guglielmo Marconi (1874–1937), failed his university entrance exam. Nevertheless, after studying research by the greatest scientists of the day, he developed one of the most influential technologies of the nineteenth and twentieth centuries. Radio brought new flexibility and speed-of-sound transmission to long-distance communications and also brought the ability to send messages quickly from one broadcaster to many listeners. Thus, it became an important technology for spreading news and propaganda (political messages). Radio played a crucial role in helping the Nazis conquer and control other nations in the period leading up to World War II; the airwaves became one of the most important wartime battlegrounds.

Radio waves had uses other than carrying speech signals. Around the time Marconi was standing on the coast of England looking toward Canada, American engineer Reginald Fessenden (1866–1932) developed the first "wireless" telephone—it sent and received calls by radio waves. Popularized by the emergency services, the military, and taxi operators, radiotelephones gradually evolved into cellular phones; in their modern form, cellular (or "cell") phones were patented in 1973 by electrical engineer Martin Cooper (1928–). Radio was also the underlying technology that led engineers to devise ways of broadcasting pictures through the air—thus television was born. Numerous inventors were involved in developing television cameras (which converted pictures into electrical signals) and television sets (which turned the electrical signals back into pictures), but modern, electronic color television sets were actually pioneered by Hungarian-born American engineer Peter Goldmark (1906–1977) in the 1930s. Not all the important advances were made by scientists. The way in which cell phones and other wireless technologies share different radio frequencies owes much to a system called **spread-spectrum communications**, originally developed for military use by 1940s' movie star Hedy Lamarr (1913–2000).

The Marvel of Still and Moving Pictures

During the nineteenth century, scientists not only learned how to record sound for posterity but also discovered how to "store" light with the development of photography. As long ago as the fourth century BCE, the Chinese developed a way of making images that later became known as a **camera obscura**. Although they could create images, they had no way of storing them.

Such storage technology was born in 1827 when French physicist Joseph Niépce (1765–1833) found he could record an image on a metal plate covered with bitumen (a kind of thick, black tar). This rather crude technique, which took eight hours to make a single photograph, was soon superseded by a better method called the **daguerreotype**, after the French artist who worked closely with Niépce to develop it, Louis Daguerre (1789–1851). William Henry Fox Talbot (1800–1877), an Englishman, improved photography further when he developed the negative–positive process still used today. In his method, paper coated with silver-based chemicals was exposed to light to produce a "negative" image of the scene being photographed, with light areas looking dark and vice versa; this negative was then "developed" (placed in various chemical baths) and used to print the scene in the "positive." Others substantially improved on Talbot's method in the years that followed, making sharper pictures that could be taken in much less time, more easily, and with less mess. Ultimately, in 1883, an American bank clerk, George Eastman (1854–1932), worked out a way of capturing photographs on plastic coated with light-sensitive chemicals. So the modern "film" was born; after Eastman invented his portable Kodak camera five years later, photography would soon become a hobby that almost anyone could enjoy. It was another example of technology gradually moving from scientists, specialists, and inventors into the hands of ordinary people.

Almost all people have desired entertainment—and photography provided that, too, in the form of motion pictures. Movies were born in 1893 when Thomas Edison's assistant, William Dickson (1860–1937), developed a mechanism that could pull a long reel of film through a camera called a kinetograph and take rapid-sequence photographs as it did so. When these many individual photographs, or frames, were later viewed in sequence at high speed in a matching film viewer or kinetoscope, the viewer's brain was tricked into seeing them as a single moving picture. Only one person at a time could

Communication Facts

- Between 1920 and 1970, the average number of long-distance telephone conversations per day grew from 1.5 million to 26.8 million.

- In 1946, the first year the US government tracked the data, the United States had eight thousand television sets.

- In 2000, daily newspapers in the United States totaled 1,480, with a circulation of more than fifty-five million.

- In 2012, sales of e-books surpassed sales of hardcover books, indicating a shift in traditional book-buying techniques.

view the kinetoscope, but it inspired two French brothers, Auguste Lumière (1862–1954) and Louis Lumière (1864–1948), to develop a better instrument, one that could project a film onto a wall for many people to view simultaneously. In 1894, the Lumières invented the Cinématographe (movie projector), and the following year they opened the world's first movie theater. Telegraphs and telephones may have changed the speed and convenience of communication, but photographs and movies changed its nature. They allowed people

Today, many people use technology such as a tablet, pictured here, to communicate with friends and family around the world.

to communicate and share human emotions in a way that had never previously been possible.

The Future of Communicating

All of these major strands in communications technology—from written language and books to radio and motion pictures—started life as separate inventions: written language was distinctly separate from spoken language, and pictures were different from words. From the mid-twentieth century onward, the spread of **digital technology** made possible the convergence of all these forms of information technology.

A key development was the user-friendly personal computer, which first appeared in the mid-1970s, pioneered by, among others, Steve Wozniak (1950–) and Steve Jobs (1955–2011), the founders of Apple Inc. Based on digital technology, personal computers gave individuals the power to store large volumes of information, edit it quickly and easily, and send it rapidly to others anywhere in the world. No other invention in history has had so much impact on the volume of information people store, process, and exchange and the speed with which they do so.

Since the beginning of the twenty-first century, people have been able to take digital photographs with a cell phone and e-mail them to friends, who edit the photographs on a laptop and print them with an ordinary computer printer or post them on the web, the information-sharing part of the Internet invented in 1989 by Tim Berners-Lee (1955–). Now, people can even take, edit, and upload photos right on their smartphones. All the above is possible because people now largely generate, store, process, and exchange information in digital form. The corporate world has taken notice. For example, although it was founded as a computer company, Apple launched the iPod music player in 2001; the iPhone in 2007; and its tablet, the iPad, in 2010. Many other companies have tried to compete with Apple. Google, Amazon, and Samsung have also made their own music players, smartphones, and tablets. The trend to become the leader of technological innovation continues to challenge companies in corporate and consumer markets. The future of technology is constantly changing and encouraging new ideas. How people will communicate twenty, forty, one hundred years from now depends on advances being made today by men and women around the world. One day, you might even be involved.

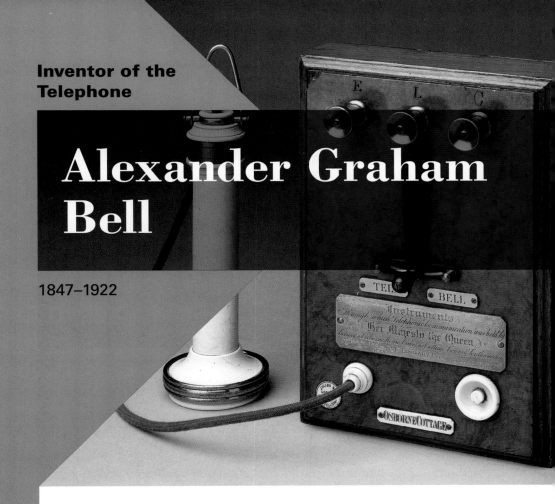

Inventor of the Telephone

Alexander Graham Bell

1847–1922

One of the most important inventions of the nineteenth century was that of the telephone. Since its beginning, the telephone's influence over communication has been great and has revolutionized the way people speak to one another over long distances. The man often attributed as its inventor, Alexander Graham Bell, developed it at the age of twenty-nine. His story is one of determination, mixed with rivalry and dispute. Over a century has passed since Bell patented the telephone, yet some people do not think he deserves credit for the invention. Still, he is remembered as one of the most influential inventors in recent times, and the telephone is one of the most essential developments in modern society.

An Inventor's Beginnings

Alexander Graham Bell was born in Edinburgh, Scotland, in 1847. Even before his birth, he seemed almost destined to make his name working in the field of human speech. His father and grandfather, both also named Alexander Bell, were tutors of speech and teachers of the deaf. His father wrote a pioneering textbook on **elocution** that was reprinted almost two hundred times.

Alexander Graham Bell, ca. 1901

Defining the Problem

The study of sound soon became the young Bell's obsession; one of his earliest memories was sitting in a field trying to hear wheat growing. His mother was profoundly deaf, but Bell discovered she could understand his words if he pressed his lips to her head so the vibrations were transmitted directly through the bones of her skull. Bell had little formal education and gained most of his knowledge through just this kind of curiosity and experiment. His first invention—a device for cleaning wheat, made when he was just eleven—was unconnected with sound. Another early invention—a speaking machine with bellows for lungs and a cotton and rubber "mouth"—set him on the path that would ultimately lead to the telephone.

Tragedy struck in 1870 when Bell's older brother, Melville, contracted tuberculosis and died. His younger brother had died of the same disease, and doctors thought Alexander was at risk of death also. Bell's father decided to relocate the family to Canada in August 1870, when Bell was twenty-three. There his son's health rapidly improved. After moving south to Boston in 1871, Bell embarked on a career teaching deaf children. He established his own school for the deaf the following year; when Boston University absorbed the school in 1873, he became its professor of vocal **physiology** and elocution.

Designing the Solution

During the next several years, Bell carried out his most important work: the experiments in converting speech into electrical impulses and from these impulses back into a sound that would lead to the telephone. Bell built his "ear phonoautograph" by connecting a bristle brush to the bones of a dead man's ear. When Bell spoke into the ear, the bones picked up the sound vibrations and made the brush wobble so that it recorded a trace on a piece of glass. Such experiments were part of what enabled Bell to develop his telephone in 1876.

In the early twenty-first century—when a single fiber-optic cable can carry spoken words, music, movies, and Internet data simultaneously—we may have trouble appreciating just how revolutionary the telephone was. In the 1870s, the telegraph was the only means of sending long-distance messages quickly from place to place. A system of electric cables usually stretching alongside railroad lines, the telegraph sent and received messages one letter at a time using a series of long and short electrical pulses called Morse code. Although we may now consider the telegraph to be slow and laborious, in the nineteenth century it was cutting-edge technology. Then, even electricity was new and quite unknown to most people.

Applying the Solution

When people first saw the telephone in action, it must have seemed like magic. How else could one explain the curious new device that carried speech from one place to another using nothing more than a thin metal wire? The greatest scientists of the day were astonished and delighted. Seeing a demonstration at the American Centennial Exposition in June 1876, Britain's William Thomson (Lord Kelvin) described it as "the most wonderful thing in America." Oliver Lodge, the distinguished British physicist who helped to invent radio, agreed; years later, he wrote, "The telephone has become so familiar that one forgets the wonder of it … No-one could imagine the extreme simplicity of the invention."

Bell was in great demand to demonstrate his new telephone. At the Centennial Exposition, he had demonstrated it to Emperor Dom

Pedro of Brazil; two years later, he showed it to England's Queen Victoria. For Bell, however, the telephone was no mere parlor room curiosity—it was a vision of the future. As he wrote to his father in 1876, "The day is coming when telegraph wires will be laid on to houses just like water or gas—and friends will converse with each other without leaving home."

Bell's Many Inventions

Most of Bell's inventions used science and technology to solve pressing human problems and meet pressing human needs. The telephone was no exception. When Oliver Lodge heard Bell demonstrate the telephone in the 1870s, he noted, "Bell spoke with the most beautiful enunciation … It was a pleasure to listen to him. He had taught many deaf people to speak and so it seemed appropriate that he should teach inorganic matter also [by devising the telephone]." Within four years, the significance of this far-reaching invention was recognized by the French government, which awarded Bell its 50,000-franc ($10,000) Volta prize for pioneering work in the field of electricity. Bell used the money to establish a laboratory in Washington, DC, in 1880. He set up a similar "invention factory" at Beinn Bhreagh, on Cape Breton Island in Nova Scotia, several years later.

Bell believed passionately in teamwork, and his laboratories, staffed with enthusiastic young engineers, helped him to explore other fields and pioneer other inventions. Predictably, his team invented many devices related to sound. One was the photophone (a telephone that could transmit speech in a beam of light—a forerunner of modern fiber-optic communication and cell phones). Another was the audiometer, which could measure the sensitivity of a person's hearing. Building on Edison's invention of the phonograph, Bell also developed a way of storing impressions of sound waves on a rotating wax cylinder that anticipated other sound-recording inventions, from the gramophone to the compact disc.

Physical inventions were not Bell's only contributions to society. In 1880, Bell helped found the journal *Science* to promote new discoveries. An interest in teaching geography led him to cofound the

National Geographic Society, for which he served as president from 1896 to 1904.

In 1877, Bell married Mabel Hubbard, one of his deaf pupils from Boston. Hubbard's father, Gardiner Green Hubbard, was a strong opponent of the powerful Western Union Telegraph Company and soon became Bell's major financial backer. By 1880, Bell and his wife had two daughters. Both of Bell's sons, one born in 1881 and the other in 1883, died in infancy.

Bell had been preoccupied with sound since he was a boy, and his lifelong commitment to helping the deaf ultimately led him to study eugenics (a controversial forerunner of modern genetics that aimed to demonstrate that careful choice of parents could eliminate diseases and improve humankind). One of Bell's most important legacies was the Alexander Graham Bell Association for the Deaf and Hard of Hearing, founded in 1890, a society that still promotes education for the deaf.

Leaping from one invention to another throughout his life, Bell's mind was constantly in motion. In the 1890s he turned his attention to the problem of making an aircraft, about a decade before the Wright brothers achieved the first powered human flight. Bell did not invent flight; archaeologists believe the ancient Nazcas, who lived in Peru around 100 BCE to 700 CE, may have been the first people to take to the air. Yet Bell was certainly a pioneer, combining his knowledge of aerodynamics (the science of how air flows around moving objects) with decades of practical experiments to make many innovative flying machines.

In the 1890s, Bell began experimenting with models of helicopters. Soon afterward he started building elaborate box-shaped kites, based on a strong but lightweight structure called a tetrahedron. He hoped his kites would be strong enough to support a person's weight. He achieved success with his tetrahedrons in 1907 after many failures. The same year, Bell cofounded the Aerial Experiment Association to develop improved motor-driven airplanes. In 1909, the group's plane, *Silver Dart*, made a record-breaking half-mile flight at a speed of 40 miles per hour (64 kilometers per hour)—over ten times faster than the Wright brothers had flown at Kitty Hawk five years earlier.

One of Bell's finest achievements involved flight of a very different kind. Always a visionary, Bell had begun to consider how wartime boats could be made fast enough to pursue submarines, which moved more swiftly underwater. His insight was to combine what he had learned from aircraft with existing boat technology. The result was a hydrodrome (now known as a hydrofoil), which used a set of four submerged wings (or foils) to lift it clear of the water so it could go faster. On September 9, 1919, his 60-foot-long (18 meter) HD-4 hydrodrome raced along at over 70 miles per hour (113 kmh)—a world water speed

Did Bell Invent the Telephone?

Antonio Meucci

Bound up in controversy for more than a century, the telephone is perhaps the most disputed invention in history. One rival, Elisha Gray (1835–1901), a professor, filed a similar patent application just two hours after Bell. His claims and those of others, including Thomas Edison, noted that Bell had not produced an actual working telephone before writing his patent. Another inventor, Amos E. Dolbear (1837–1910), claimed to have invented the telephone before Bell and sold the rights to the powerful Western Union Telegraph Company. A lengthy court battle between Bell's firm and Western Union was eventually resolved in Bell's favor, as was another battle with Edison.

Yet history has almost forgotten the man with the best claim of all: Antonio Meucci (1808–1889), an Italian-born record that was not broken until 1963. It was Bell's last great invention and one of his most impressive.

The First Telephone Conversation

The first words uttered over the telephone were, "Mr. Watson! Come here! I want to see you!" When Alexander Graham Bell said this to his assistant Thomas Watson on March 10, 1876, the two men were in different rooms. The words traveled not as sound waves through the air but as pulses of electricity down a cable. A remarkable invention had been born.

theater technician widely thought to have invented the telephone while living in Havana, Cuba, in the 1840s. Meucci immigrated to New York in 1850 to promote his invention, which he later called his "teletrofono." In the 1850s, when his wife became paralyzed, he even wired up the rooms in his house with such a device so she could speak to him in his workshop.

Meucci's English was poor, he struggled to find backers, and he could not afford to protect his invention properly with a patent, which then cost $250. In 1871, he filed a less expensive form of protection called a patent caveat. Though it cost only $10, he could not afford to renew it after 1874—a failure that allowed Bell to file a full patent on the telephone in 1876. When Meucci found out, he fought Bell in court in 1886, and the US government moved to quash Bell's patent the following year on the grounds of fraud and misrepresentation. It even came to light that Bell had carried out experiments in the very laboratory where Meucci had stored his own materials.

Meucci was old, impoverished, and unable to continue fighting. When he died in 1889 the case was dropped. However, the controversy never went away. Finally in 2002, the US Congress passed a bill noting Meucci's "extraordinary and tragic" career and recognized him as the true inventor of the telephone.

Like many great inventors, Bell was a genius at fusing together the best technology and science of his day. He did not set out to invent the telephone, however. His initial goal had been to improve the telegraph by finding a way to send multiple messages along a wire at the same time. He was also keenly aware of the latest scientific research showing that sound could be turned into electricity, and vice versa. In 1854, a French telegraphist, Charles Bourseul (1829–1912), had outlined the idea of sending speech down a wire: "I ask myself … if speech itself couldn't also be transmitted by electricity; in a word, if we couldn't speak in Vienna and be heard in Paris." Bourseul never actually achieved this, though others came close. In 1861, German teacher Johann Philipp Reis (1834–1874) built a crude sound-carrying device using, among other things, a knitting needle, a cork, and a piece of sausage skin—but it could not transmit speech. The great German physicist Hermann Helmholtz (1821–1894) also transmitted sound along wires; he used electricity to make tuning forks vibrate so they "sang" different vowel sounds.

Such work strongly influenced Bell, whose invention was born of a combination of thought, insight, and experiment. Building on the work of Helmholtz, Bell reasoned that if vowel sounds could be carried by wire, so could any other sounds. Unlike other inventors who were working on the problem of sending multiple messages by telegraph, Bell realized he could use the same piece of equipment both to send and to receive messages. Nevertheless, the telephone was born as much by accident as by design. In June 1875, Bell and Watson were testing a telegraph that used a type of electromagnetic contact called a reed relay to send and receive signals. When Watson accidentally plucked one of the reeds, Bell heard the same sound in another room. Realizing what had happened, he rushed in to his colleague shouting: "Watson, what did you do then? Don't change anything!" Within a short time, the two men had rearranged the apparatus and produced a crude telephone that could transmit their voices reliably, not just by accident.

Within three months, Bell had drafted a patent application and submitted it in February 1876. The patent (US Patent No. 174,465) was granted in March of that year for: "The method of, and apparatus for, transmitting vocal or other sounds telegraphically." With the exception of cell phones, which carry calls using radio waves, virtually every telephone has worked this way ever since.

Bell remained a prolific inventor until the day he died, on August 2, 1922. Every telephone connected to the Bell system was switched off during his funeral service—a fitting mark of respect for the man whose most significant invention enabled spoken words to cross the globe.

The Impact of the Solution on Society

Whether Bell deserves the credit for inventing the telephone (see box, Did Bell Invent the Telephone?), he certainly played a key part in promoting it toward the end of the nineteenth century. His high-profile demonstrations throughout the world rapidly convinced people that the telephone was a serious piece of technology, and the Bell Telephone Company was formed in 1877 to capitalize on it. The company grew rapidly and in 1885 took its now familiar name of American Telephone & Telegraph (AT&T). Just ten years after Bell's invention, the United States boasted over 150,000 telephones, with an estimated 50,000 more in Europe and Russia. Today, nearly every household in the US has at least one phone, many of them cellular.

The telephone was unquestionably one of the most far-reaching inventions of the nineteenth century, and it has only grown in importance since. Amplifying circuits, which boost electric signals so they can travel farther, soon made long-distance calls possible. Automated exchanges, which were invented in 1889 by Kansas City undertaker Almon Strowger (1839–1902), allowed calls to be routed faster, farther, and more reliably. Innovations such as coaxial cable—many thin copper wires packed into a thick outer casing—invented in 1936, allowed telephone cables to carry thousands of calls; tiny fiber-optic cables currently allow millions of calls to be carried at once.

Although Bell developed the telephone only to carry speech, from the mid-twentieth century onward telephone capabilities expanded. Soon they were able to send documents via a fax machine, to link computers together using special telephone adapters called modems, and ultimately to connect hundreds of millions of computers to the Internet. In the 1970s, a new form of telephone was born: the cellular phone. This phone allowed people to receive calls wherever they happened to be by using radio waves instead of wires. Perhaps if Bell had been alive to see this take on his patented invention, he would have thought them similar to his photophone—an invention that carried phone calls in beams of light. Regardless, the telephone has stood the test of time and continues to influence the world as one of humanity's greatest inventions

Timeline

1847
Alexander Graham Bell born in Edinburgh, Scotland

1870
Bell family relocates to Canada

1871
Bell moves to Boston and begins working as a teacher for the deaf

1876
Bell invents the telephone

1877
Bell Telephone Company is founded

1880
Bell establishes a laboratory in Washington, DC

1909
Bell's plane, *The Silver Dart,* flies at 40 miles per hour (64 kmh)

1919
Bell's hydrodrome captures the water speed record

1922
Bell dies

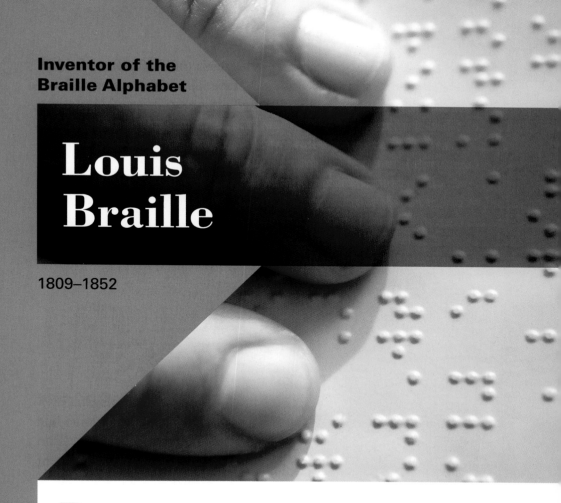

Louis Braille

1809–1852

Prior to the invention of a new form of writing, blind people had few opportunities for education or advancement. That began to change in 1824, when Louis Braille invented a way of writing with raised dots. This communication method, named after Braille, opened doors for blind people and helped gain them the recognition they deserved.

A Difficult Beginning

Louis Braille was born on January 4, 1809, in Coupvray, a small village in Seine-et-Marne, France. Louis's father, Simon-René Braille, was a saddle maker who ran his business from a large workshop attached to the family's stone cottage. As a toddler,

An illustration of Louis Braille

Louis must have played in the workshop, watching his father cutting leather and working it with his collection of strangely shaped tools.

When he was three years old, Louis got into the workshop when his father was away. Having seen his father use the tools, he decided to try the same thing himself. He picked up a sharp object and started playing with it, but his hand slipped and he poked himself in the eye. Although the wound was not that serious, it soon became infected. A local healer used lily water as a treatment; an eye doctor in a nearby town tried other remedies. None of these cures worked, and Louis lost sight in both eyes.

His desperate parents persuaded the local school to let Louis sit in on classes and listen. When the government no longer allowed blind children to be taught this way, Louis's teacher and priest helped him win a scholarship to a special school, the Royal Institute for Blind Children in Paris, and Louis entered in February 1819.

Louis was miserable at the institute. Despite its prestige, the school was a damp, run-down building. The children had one bath a month and drank muddy water direct from the nearby Seine. The director of the school, Sébastien Guillié, thought blind people were "degraded beings, condemned to vegetate on the earth," and the children spent most of their time sewing and mending slippers, chairs, hospital sheets, and the like to support their stay there. Because Guillié loved music, the pupils did get to play instruments. Louis learned to play the piano, cello, and organ, and his recitals, in churches throughout Paris, earned him great fame.

Defining the Problem

In 1821, Guillié was fired for misconduct. His replacement, André Pignier, was kinder to the children and tried to improve their lives. He introduced weekly walks where teachers led pupils, all holding onto a long rope, to favorite gardens, museums, and churches.

One day, Pignier invited the school's elderly founder, Valentin Haüy, back for a ceremony to thank him for dedicating his life to the blind. One of Haüy's inventions was a system for helping blind children to read. He pressed dampened paper onto raised letters so their shapes pushed up through the paper in relief. When the paper dried, it held the letter shapes and blind children could read them with their fingers. It was not a very practical system, as the letters were huge and the books enormous, but it must have seemed like a godsend to blind children who had no other way of reading. The school owned

Understanding Braille

Each letter in Braille is written using a pattern of six closely spaced dots, a bit like those on dice, only standing out in relief and arranged in three rows of two. The first ten letters (*A* through *J*) use only the top four dots; the next ten letters (*K* through *T*) repeat the same pattern but add one more dot underneath; the remaining letters generally add two more dots underneath. Numbers are written using the same pattern as the ten letters *A* through *J* but preceded with a special number sign (#). A more advanced form of Braille (called grade 2 or contracted Braille) is much faster to read because entire words are represented by just one or two letters.

Blind people write in Braille using a slate. This is a hinged piece of metal or plastic into which the blind person slips a sheet of paper. The slate has a grid of about twenty-eight rectangular-shaped cells, and each one of these is punched with six tiny holes. The blind person presses a pointed stylus into the holes to make different letters in the cells, then gradually moves the slate down the page. This process is slow and laborious, so many blind people use computer equipment instead. Their computers translate ordinary letters into Braille and use special printers, known as Braille embossers, to print out what they have written.

Braille books are huge compared with books used by sighted people. Although Braille letters are small, they are still larger than ordinary print and, because of the raised dots, the paper is also much thicker. Using either slates or Braille embossers, blind people can write on both sides of the paper. In this technique, known as interpoint, the letters are spaced so the dots on either side of the page do not interfere with one another. Even so, a large book, such as a dictionary, can still take up an entire bookshelf when printed in Braille.

fourteen books printed using Haüy's method, and Louis Braille, eager to educate himself, soon read them all. Braille was excited about and inspired by meeting the great man whose invention was helping him.

The school had another important visitor, an army officer named Charles Barbier. He had invented a system called night-writing that allowed soldiers to pass messages to one another in the dark without lighting torches and giving away their position to the enemy. Barbier's system involved punching dots and dashes into cardboard so they stood out in relief. The soldiers agreed on a code: one pattern might mean "advance," while another meant "send reinforcements." When Barbier realized night-writing could help the blind, he contacted Pignier to arrange a demonstration.

Designing the Solution

Louis Braille was one of the first civilians to try out Barbier's system. He thought it was wonderful because it was faster than using Valentin Haüy's embossed letters. However, it was hard to learn because it was based on the sounds of letters, not the letters themselves. It was also slow to read because it used twelve raised dots to represent each letter. Braille thought he could do better and started to experiment. By 1824, at age fifteen, he had developed an improved system using only six raised dots for each letter. Unlike Barbier, he made each pattern of dots small enough to fit under his fingertip so he could read these letters with great speed (see sidebar, Understanding Braille). Over the next few years he continued to improve his Braille alphabet, as it became known. He invented special writing "slates" to help people write in Braille and even developed a version of Braille for writing down music.

Bridging a Divide

Pignier soon made the nineteen-year-old Louis Braille a professor at the school. Braille had learned a great deal from his teachers and was determined to be kinder and more caring. His pupils were the first to try his alphabet, and their experience helped him to improve his invention. One difficulty was that children learning to read and write with Braille had no way of writing to their sighted families. So in 1841, working with another former pupil of the school, Pierre Foucault, Louis Braille invented a printing machine called a raphigraph. This used a grid of tiny raised dots to make the outlines of ordinary letters so they could be read by either blind or sighted people. It worked a bit like a mechanical typewriter—around fifty years before the first practical typewriter was developed.

Although Braille's alphabet was popular with pupils, the school staff was less enthusiastic. Most of the teachers were sighted and found Braille difficult to use. Armand Dufau, the assistant director of the college, fought the introduction of the Braille alphabet because he thought it made blind people too independent. When Dufau became the school's director, he burned all the books by Haüy and confiscated the special writing slates that Braille had developed. The pupils rebelled and carried on writing Braille in secret, pushing dots in paper using knitting needles, nails, and whatever else they could find. Eventually, Dufau was persuaded to change his mind.

A blind man reads a sign written in English and Braille.

Final Years

By now, Louis Braille was seriously ill. Conditions at the school had improved, but the place was still damp and unhealthy, and he had developed tuberculosis. In those days, the illness usually led to death. Braille's health gradually deteriorated, though it improved whenever he returned to his hometown, Coupvray. Although he was devoted to his pupils, he missed his family. In September 1847, Braille wrote his mother: "I long to see you. Living in town is boring and I shall be happy to breathe the country air and walk with you through the vineyards."

Braille died on January 6, 1852, at only forty-three—but that was not the end of his story. He was buried in Coupvray, and his body remained there for one hundred years, until 1952. By then, his importance as a great inventor was recognized and people demanded that he be buried in Paris instead. His body was exhumed (dug up), and his hands were cut off and returned to a tomb in Coupvray, while the rest of his body was taken to the Pantheon, a famous church where France's national heroes are buried. At the funeral service in Paris in 1952, his coffin was followed down the street by hundreds of blind people tapping white canes.

The Impact of the Solution on Society

Braille's alphabet took a great deal of time to catch on—even France did not fully adopt the system until two years after Louis Braille died. Almost forty years then passed before Braille's system was taken up by other countries (Austria, Belgium, Denmark, England, Germany, Scotland, and Spain). In the United States, a rival system called New York Point was initially more popular, though Braille was universally adopted in 1917. (There was still some resistance, however; the head of one Missouri school for the blind argued that Braille should not be used because it was not "pleasing to the eye.") Finally, in 1949, the United Nations agreed that Braille should be modified for use in more countries. After that, it soon became a worldwide, universal written language for the blind.

Arguably, Braille's invention was not original: he got his idea from earlier work by Valentin Haüy and Charles Barbier. However, unlike these two well-meaning men, Louis Braille had been blind almost from birth, so he knew what blind people really needed. His adaptation of their ideas made Braille quicker to read, which made it popular and opened up the world of written communication to the blind. Thanks to Braille, blind people can read books, write letters, and share knowledge just like anyone else.

Today, while many people still use Braille to read and write, there are other options for them to experience the written and spoken word. New technologies have benefited the blind and partially sighted communities, and more societies have become aware of the needs of people with disabilities. Computers and other electronic devices now have software that reads text onscreen for the user. Likewise, many places are as accessible to blind and partially sighted people as any-where else. For his contribution to these communities, of which he was a part, Louis Braille will always be remembered and uplifted.

Timeline

1809
Louis Braille born in Coupvray, France

1812
Braille has an accident that causes him to become blind

1819
Braille enrolls at the Royal Institute for Blind Children

1821
André Pignier becomes head of the institute

1824
Braille develops his alphabet

1828
Braille becomes a teacher at the institute

1841
Braille invents the raphigraph

1852
Braille dies of tuberculosis

Inventor of the Fax Machine

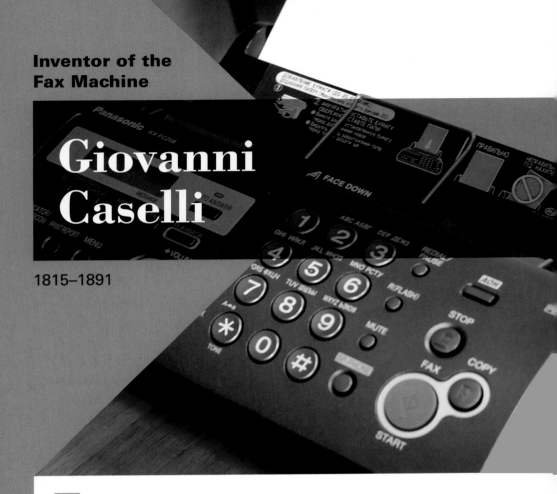

Giovanni Caselli

1815–1891

Technologies such as the telegraph and telephone advanced the way people communicated with each other. However, messages and sounds were not the only information people needed to send over long distances; documents and images sometimes were needed more quickly than the mail could carry them. It became clear that a new mechanism to transfer these items was needed. The person to solve this problem was Giovanni Caselli. He became the first person to invent a device that could transmit information and images in a document down a telegraph line to be printed out at the other end. However, his invention took time to gain popularity—as long as one hundred years. Once it did, the fax (short for facsimile) machine became one of the most widely used devices of the twentieth century.

Beginnings

Details of Caselli's early life are sketchy. He was born in 1815 in Siena, in the Italian region of Tuscany, where he studied science and literature. In his mid-twenties, he became a teacher. Between 1841 and 1849, he was living in the **duchy** of Modena. When the people rioted for a change of government in the 1850s, Caselli took part in the disturbance. As a result, he lost his job and was expelled from the duchy.

Giovanni Caselli envisioned the fax machine long before it became practical to use.

Defining the Problem

Soon afterward, he moved to the University of Florence to teach physics. Around this time, Samuel Morse (1791–1872) developed his telegraph: a simple on-off switch that could send messages between two places down a length of ordinary electric cable. The telegraph captured Caselli's imagination, but he found it slow and laborious to use, and he wondered why it could not transmit pictures as well as words. Caselli, who had saved lots of money working as a teacher in Modena, now began to spend it on experiments to develop an improved telegraph.

First Attempts

Caselli was not the first to turn his attention to this problem. In the 1840s, Scottish inventor Alexander Bain (1811–1877) patented a "chemical telegraph" that could send and receive images as well as words. At one end, the sender wrote or drew a message on a piece of chemically treated paper. A metal stylus traced over the pattern, converted it into a series of electrical pulses, and transmitted them down a telegraph wire to a receiving apparatus at the other end, where the pulses were printed back onto paper.

Bain's device was demonstrated in France to a committee of scientists and politicians; it transmitted 282 words in just fifty-two seconds—around seven times faster than the Morse telegraph. Although it caught on to a limited extent in Britain, it never really stood a chance in the United States. When Samuel Morse saw a demonstration, he immediately understood the threat of Bain's device. He discovered that Bain's chemical telegraph infringed his own patent and took legal action to stop his rival. Bain appealed, and the injunction was eventually overturned by the Supreme Court, but by that point Morse's telegraph was already well established, while Bain's promising invention was condemned to obscurity.

Designing the Solution

About a decade after Bain's experiments, Caselli began to develop his own chemical telegraph in Florence. The grand duke of Tuscany took an interest and encouraged Caselli to continue. In 1857, Caselli moved to Paris and began collaborating with telegraph engineer Paul Gustave Froment (1815–1865). Aware of Bain's invention, Caselli used some similar ideas in his own invention, which became known as the pantelegraph. Nothing was less like a modern fax machine than this elaborate contraption of cast iron standing more than 6 feet (1.8 m) high and with a huge pendulum similar to the one in a grandfather clock.

To transmit a message, the sender had to write or draw on a thin sheet of tin using special ink made from a fatty substance that did not conduct electricity. The tin sheet was wrapped around a curved plate and a moving stylus was scanned over it. Where the tin had no ink, the stylus passed electricity through the plate and generated a short telegraph pulse; where lines were written or drawn in the fatty ink, the electricity was interrupted, so no pulse was generated. Thus, the stylus transformed the document into an on-off pattern of pulses that could be transmitted on a telegraph wire.

At the receiving end, Caselli installed a similar apparatus. Instead of a scanning mechanism, however, the receiver had a chemical printing mechanism with a moving needle. As the electrical pulses arrived, the needle jerked back and forth, reproducing the words and pictures scanned at the other end. The main technical problem Caselli faced was synchronizing the sender's apparatus with the receiver's. The pendulums provided a simple timing mechanism that allowed the two pieces of apparatus to work in tandem.

Applying the Solution

Initially, Caselli's invention was a success. In 1860, the French emperor Napoleon III was so excited that he even visited Caselli's workshop for a demonstration. When he saw how well the machine

The Workings of a Fax Machine

Caselli's pantelegraph was a mechanical marvel of cogs, wheels, levers, and pendulums; fax machines in the twentieth and twenty-first centuries are almost entirely electronic. While the pantelegraph used separate machines for sending and receiving documents, a modern fax can do either job.

During sending, a document feeds slowly through the machine. As it does, it curves around a roller and past a narrow, bright beam of light. The light reflects off the page into a light-detecting unit (photocell). White parts of the page (where there is no ink) reflect most light and cause the photocell to generate a burst of electricity. Black, inked parts of the page reflect little or no light, so the photocell generates no electricity. Thus, as the page scans through, the photocell generates a series of electrical pulses that correspond to the pattern of ink on the page.

These pulses travel down the telephone line to a fax machine at the other end. When the machine receives the pulses, it decodes them and figures out the patterns of light and dark they represent. A printer unit reproduces this pattern on paper that feeds through the receiver's machine. Just as in Caselli's original pantelegraph, two modern fax machines work in exact synchronization; these days, they do so electronically, not by using giant swinging pendulums.

worked, he granted Caselli permission to use French telegraph lines to develop his machine further. A full-scale trial, sending messages between Paris and the town of Amiens, followed several months later. The following year, Caselli officially registered his invention. By 1865, it was in full-scale operation between Paris and Lyon, transmitting five thousand documents during its first year. In France, Caselli was hailed as a hero, and Napoleon awarded him the Legion of Honor. Parisian scientists and engineers even formed a Pantelegraph Society to share their ideas and promote the device. The invention rapidly

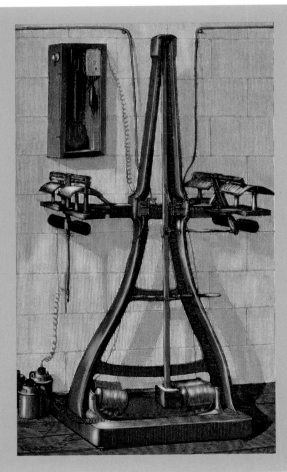

The pantelegraph, Caselli's version of a fax machine

spread to England, Italy, and Russia, where it was used to send messages between palaces in St. Petersburg and Moscow.

The novelty soon wore off, however. Users found the machine clumsy and difficult to operate, and it was expensive to send messages. Quite often, the sending and receiving apparatus got out of step and transmissions became garbled or illegible. Although the pantelegraph could transmit any kind of document, people tended to use it purely for sending drawn images, which limited its market. Adoption of the invention was so slow that investors lost interest. Before long, the pantelegraph fell into disuse and Caselli was forced to give up on it.

Reinventing Caselli's Invention

Although Caselli's invention fell into obscurity, his idea was still viable. In the early decades of the twentieth century, document-transmitting machines were reinvented using entirely different technology. In 1924, Richard Ranger (1899–1961), an electrical engineer at Radio Corporation of America (RCA), developed a machine that could send pictures from one place to another using radio waves. On November 29, 1924, Ranger's machine, the wireless photoradiogram, transmitted the first fax photograph—a picture of President Calvin Coolidge—from New York City to London, England.

The same year, American Telephone & Telegraph (AT&T) developed what was then called "telephotography" or sometimes "phototelegraphy": a way of sending photographs down ordinary telephone lines. In 1925, AT&T's Bell Laboratories gave the first public demonstration of this new technology, which took seven minutes to transmit a single image.

The Impact of the Solution on Society

For much of the twentieth century, written documents were sent between distant places using teleprinters and telex machines. Like electric typewriters, these machines used pulses of electricity to send messages back and forth on ordinary telegraph and telephone lines. In the 1970s, the invention of the computer chip (microprocessor) led to the development of the modern, electronic fax machine. This remained the most popular method of sending documents over long distances until the mid-1990s. Today, fax machines still operate around the world, but their use and sales have severely declined. This is due to other, faster devices such as e-mail taking the place of these electronic mechanisms.

In his lifetime, Caselli invented other devices: a missile that, when fired from a ship, would automatically return to its firing position if it missed its target; a speed-measuring instrument for steam locomotives; and a hydraulic press. However, the pantelegraph was undoubtedly his greatest invention, and its failure remained a deep disappointment to him until his death in Florence in 1891. Still, the beginnings of the device remained, and his creation was one that continued to be in use for well over a century.

Timeline

1815
Giovanni Caselli born in Siena, Italy

1857
Caselli moves to Paris and collaborates with telegraph engineer Paul Gustave Froment

1860
Napoleon III visits Caselli's workshop for a demonstration of his pantelegraph

1861
Caselli officially registers the pantelegraph

1865
The pantelegraph starts full-scale operations between Paris and Lyon

1891
Caselli dies

Developer of the Cell Phone

Martin Cooper

1928–

While the nineteenth century saw the creation of many noted inventions, perhaps the two greatest of that period were the telephone and the radio. As these devices improved over the years, the two combined to form the cellular phone. The cellular, or "cell," phone has been one of the greatest inventions in modern times. Use of the phone has grown since it was developed in the 1970s. Today, nearly six billion cell phones are used worldwide. Many people played a part in developing the cell phone, but an American named Martin Cooper usually gets credit for making it a reality.

Early Life of an Inventor

When Martin Cooper was born on December 26, 1928, the modern electronic tools that we now take for granted—personal computers, color televisions, tablets, and iPods—had yet to be invented. "It's really embarrassing," he recalled later. "The television did not become commercial until I was past my teen years." Growing up in Chicago, Cooper—like many children did in those days—entertained himself by reading books, especially science fiction.

At that time the most exciting new technology was radio. People called it "wireless" and thought of it mostly in connection with radio programs and, later, with television (because radio waves are also used to transmit the images seen on a television screen). Few people had any idea that radio had other uses. Cooper believed, however, that radio was the future. After earning a degree in electrical engineering at the Illinois Institute of Technology, he served in the navy during World War II and then joined the research department of a telecommunications company.

The Use of Radios and Telephones

The road to cellular phones began with Alexander Graham Bell's invention of the telephone in 1876. Around the same time, scientists were discovering how radio waves could send information through the air without using wires. The first person to transmit human speech by radio waves was American engineer Reginald Fessenden (1866–1932). On December 24, 1906, Fessenden used radio to send a spoken message 11 miles (17.7 km) from Brant Rock, Massachusetts, to ships in the Atlantic Ocean.

Defining the Problem

The first truly mobile phones, called radiotelephones, appeared by the 1940s; they were cumbersome radio sets carried around in emergency vehicles and taxis. In 1946, AT&T and Southwestern Bell introduced MTS (Mobile Telephone System), a commercial radio system that used five antennas and a central switching office to transmit conversations between moving vehicles. The following year, AT&T introduced a long-distance radiotelephone service between New York City and Boston.

These early systems were so popular that they had waiting lists of up to ten years to buy them. They were limited in that they could transmit only a few telephone calls simultaneously. Early radiotelephones sent and received calls on a narrow section of radio wave frequencies known as a band. This was like a pipe of limited diameter through which only a certain number of calls could squeeze at a time.

Designing the Solution

Clearly many people wanted radiotelephones. In response, the Federal Communications Commission (the FCC, a US government body that regulates telecommunications) agreed to make more frequencies available if telephone companies could find a more efficient way to

Enhancing Communication

When Alexander Graham Bell invented the telephone in 1876, he was trying to solve a specific problem: how to carry speech down a wire using electricity. The arrival of fax machines, and later the Internet, made sending all kinds of information (or data) along telephone wires possible. Once simply a way of carrying voices, the phone network is increasingly seen as a "multimedia pipeline" along which almost limitless information can travel.

A similar transformation has happened with cell phones. When Martin Cooper developed his first cell phone in the 1970s, it was designed for people like taxi drivers who needed to make calls on the move. The arrival of digital cell phone technology in the early 1980s made it possible to send and receive any kind of digital data between two cell phones or between a cell phone and another computer-based gadget. Thus, many cell phones now have built-in digital cameras that can send and receive photos and video clips.

use them. Two companies, AT&T Bell Labs and Motorola, took up the challenge. In the late 1960s, Bell Labs developed a system, called Metroliner, that enabled public pay telephones on trains to send and receive calls by radio. Motorola, where Martin Cooper had been working since 1954, was developing a completely mobile phone.

At Motorola, Cooper had led a team of scientists who developed walkie-talkie radios, used for the first time by the Chicago police department in 1967. Cooper's walkie-talkies were comparatively simple because only a limited number of radios were in use at once. Developing a full-scale radio telephone system was trickier. What was needed was a way of allowing many different telephones to use the same band of radio frequencies but to keep the different calls from interfering with each other.

Cooper solved this problem by using a system called "cells," which had been invented by Bell Labs in the 1960s. The idea was to place radio antennas all around a city in a honeycomb pattern. Each antenna would serve only the small area, or cell, immediately

Most can send e-mail and browse web pages. Some have built-in MP3 players, video players, digital radios, and even tiny digital televisions. Cell phones started out as mobile telephones; they have rapidly become go-anywhere, do-anything personal communicators, firing streams of digital data back and forth through the air.

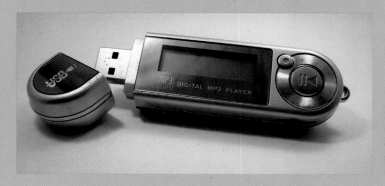

Many MP3 players, like this one, are now smaller and built into cell phones.

Martin Cooper with the first cell phone, DynaTAC, from 1973

around it, not the entire city. Neighboring cells could use the same radio frequencies, so as the number of antennas and cells increased, the number of telephones that could be used at the same time would increase also.

Motorola's first cell phone was the shape and size of a brick and weighed 28 pounds (12.7 kg). However, Cooper's team soon took advantage of new microelectronic technology to build a smaller device, the DynaTAC, which weighed only 2.8 pounds (1.27 kg). On April 3, 1973, Cooper walked through the streets of New York City to demonstrate the new phone. He decided to test it one last time and, on the spur of the moment, called his rival at Bell Labs, an engineer named Joel Engel, to boast of his achievement. Of this, the world's first cell phone conversation, Cooper said later, "I don't remember my precise words. I do remember a kind of embarrassed silence at the other end." The patent for a "radio telephone system" was granted to Martin Cooper and seven of his Motorola colleagues on September 16, 1975. Telephones had caused a revolution at the end of the nineteenth century; mobile cell phones caused a similar stir some hundred years later. By the early 1980s, Cooper's team at Motorola was running a large-scale test service in Washington, DC, and Baltimore, Maryland. DynaTAC, the world's first commercial handheld cellular phone, finally went on sale in 1984. This first-generation system weighed 28 ounces (793 g) and cost $3,995, and the battery had a one-hour life.

Applying the Solution

Technology advanced greatly during the 1980s. In Europe, twenty-six telephone manufacturers got together and launched a joint cell phone system known as Global System for Mobile Telecommunications (GSM). It used digital technology. For example, calls were transmitted not as raw sounds but as coded strings of numbers. This enabled many more telephone calls to be handled. It offered other advantages, too: digital phone calls had better sound quality, had greater protection from eavesdropping, and could send and receive short written messages (known as SMS or text messages). In the United States, the PCS (Personal Communications Services) system worked in a similar way. These systems came to be known as second-generation networks.

The Impact of the Solution on Society

In the twenty-first century, mobile networks are faster, the handsets are smaller, and all kinds of information can be sent to and from a cell phone. The development of a new kind of cell phone, the smartphone, in 2007 also led to people favoring their phones as computers rather than having two or more separate devices. In many cases, people are abandoning landlines entirely and relying on their cell phones as main outlets of communication with the rest of the world.

Several decades after making the world's first cell phone call, Martin Cooper is still too busy to retire: "Think about what the alternative is," he told one reporter. "You could sit around talking about the past and boring people to death, or you can keep active and be where the action is." In 2006, he was the chairman of his fifth start-up company, ArrayCom, which develops advanced cell phone networks. His contribution to the technological industry has been monumental, his invention something that has changed the world and challenged others to discover the next big break in technology.

Timeline

1928
Martin Cooper born in Chicago

1954
Cooper joins research department at Motorola

1967
Cooper's team develops walkie-talkie radios

1973
Cooper's team develops the DynaTAC

1975
Cooper's team at Motorola awarded a patent for a "radio telephone system"

2006
Cooper serves as chairman of ArrayCom

Janus Friis and Niklas Zennström

1976–
and
1966–

█t used to be that when you wanted to make a phone call, you picked up your family's rotary or touch-tone phone and made a call. As years passed and cell phones became more common, calling became easier. You could simply tell the phone to dial a specific person by name. Calling someone in your local area was usually free, but making long-distance calls was costly, so most people saved those for important or special occasions. Nowadays, though, you don't have to pay a dime to make a call to anyone, anywhere. Well, that is, anyone anywhere who uses Skype, the network-calling brainchild of Janus Friis and Niklas Zennström. Skype added a new dimension to communication and quickly became so pervasive that its name was made into a verb—"I'll Skype you to discuss this

Janus Friis (*left*) and Niklas Zennström (*right*), cofounders of Skype

tomorrow." As Doug Aamoth, technical editor for *TIME*, says, "When you become a verb, you know you've made it." Friis and Zennström changed the way people communicate and inspired many other similar inventions, such as Apple's FaceTime function, that have transformed modern technology and the way people connect to each other.

Voyage to VoIP

Friis and Zennström developed Skype, but they weren't the first people to explore the realm of making calls over computer networks and the Internet. Two early technologies were network voice protocol, developed by Danny Cohen, and VoIP (Voice over Internet Protocol), invented by Alon Cohen (no relation to Danny, though interestingly, they are both Israeli-born) and further developed by Jeff Pulver. Danny Cohen's network voice protocol, implemented in late 1973, allowed human speech to be sent over a computer network using **packets**. In 1989, Alon Cohen founded VocalTec Communications Inc. and invented a type of audio transceiver that eventually made VoIP possible. VocalTec was the first company to offer Internet phone services—and, interestingly, was one of the first successful Internet **IPOs**.

Although Alon Cohen's contribution to VoIP is certainly critical and noteworthy, VoIP was further developed by Jeff Pulver, considered a pioneer in VoIP technology. Pulver cofounded Vonage, one of the first and biggest VoIP companies.

Network calling through VoIP gained popularity among the tech-savvy, but it wasn't used much by the general public. That is, until Skype debuted in August 2003.

Growing Up

Born in Copenhagen, Denmark, on June 26, 1976, Janus Friis isn't your typical success story. He wasn't college educated; in fact, he dropped out of high school at age sixteen and traveled around Bombay, India. Upon his return to Denmark, he started working at the help desk for one of Denmark's earliest Internet service providers (ISP). In 1996, he met Swedish-born Niklas Zennström, ten years his senior, who was the head of European telecommunications operator Tele2 in Denmark. Friis began running Tele2's customer support, and while there he and Zennström launched another Danish ISP, get2net, as well as a portal called everyday.com.

Unlike Friis, Zennström followed a more conventional path to entrepreneurial success. The son of two teachers, he graduated high school and earned a bachelor's degree in business administration and a master's degree in engineering physics from Uppsala University in Sweden, with a year spent at the University of Michigan, Ann Arbor.

When Friis and Zennström left Tele2 in 2000, Friis moved into Zennström's Amsterdam apartment. Together, the men began developing KaZaA, which they had purchased from the Estonian programmers Ahti Heinla, Priit Kasesalu, and Jaan Tallinn, who had created the technology. KaZaA was a peer-to-peer file-sharing network that allowed people to share music files, videos, and programs. It featured no central servers for the files; rather, the network allowed anyone online to share files with anyone else connected, using a file-sharing protocol called FastTrack, which Friis codesigned.

Although KaZaA was initially created by Estonian programmers, it was Friis and Zennström who tinkered with it and got it to be the most downloaded piece of software ever as of 2003.

Not Always Skype?

Little-known fact: Skype was originally called Skyper. The name was changed because Skyper wasn't available with all Internet domains—the name already belonged to a German paging service. Friis made the suggestion to drop the final letter and call their product Skype, reasoning that it could be used as a verb. Zennström agreed, later saying, "We want [the name] to become synonymous with Internet telephony. 'I'll Skype you later.'"

Friis and Zennström later used the same peer-to-peer networking concept created for KaZaA to build Skype.

Meanwhile, Zennström also founded Joltid, a software company specializing in peer-to-peer solutions and traffic-optimization technology. Likewise, he and Friis cofounded Altnet, a peer-to-peer network specializing in promotion, distribution, and payment for commercial content.

Defining the Problem

Skype is what some refer to as "disruptive technology"—that is, technology that creates a new market while disrupting an existing one. The technology Skype disrupted was traditional telephone service. For years, people had made phone calls on landlines—phones connected to telephone lines, either by a physical cord or wirelessly. Traditional phone service eventually began to stray into the digital realm in the 1950s, but it was still largely controlled by the phone company—a giant entity informally called "Ma Bell" by many.

The main problem with this technology was that it was expensive. Regardless of whether you used analog or digital phone service, it was costly, and while digital offered more features than analog, the sound quality wasn't great. Cell phones were becoming more and more popular, but they, too, were expensive, and the sound quality could be lacking. Dropped calls were numerous, and depending on the carrier used, dead spots could be common. Simply put, cell phones weren't terribly reliable, and they weren't cheap.

So Friis and Zennström set about to create a new market. They determined that they could use the network packet technology of VoIP and apply it to a peer-to-peer networking solution, such as what they had used for KaZaA. And voilà! Phone service for free, over people's existing Internet connections.

Designing the Solution

Since Skype is built on a peer-to-peer networking concept, the more people who are using the network, the more reliable it will be. So in creating Skype, Friis and Zennström knew they needed to attract a lot of users, and what's the best way to attract people to a new product? Offer them something for free!

As mentioned earlier, long-distance calling via a phone company was expensive. Before 2003, network voice protocol and VoIP solutions were available, but they weren't terribly widespread, and they weren't free. However, with the introduction of Skype, people could talk to anyone else on it and not pay a cent! What's more, because of the peer-to-peer technology used, calls from remote places didn't have to be routed through servers in more populated areas, which meant the call quality was better. As if quality calling service for free wasn't enough, Skype offered instant messaging and videoconferencing—again free among Skype users.

Applying the Solution

So how did Friis and Zennström's venture make money? After all, you can't give away something completely for free and expect to make a living. Skype allowed free video and phone calls and instant messages among Skype users but charged a modest fee for calls to and from outside phone numbers, such as landlines. Also, voicemail was considered a premium service and was available for a fee—but these fees were miniscule compared to what a phone company charged. Thus the service became extremely popular; people didn't necessarily mind sitting at their computer to make a phone call if it meant they could do so for much less money than a phone company would charge. Moreover, they didn't have to wait too long before Skype service was available on cell phones, making it even more convenient.

Meanwhile, Friis and Zennström's gamble with the "free" service paid off. The for-pay portions of Skype generated more than $18 million in sales in the company's first fourteen months. Since these premium services were prepaid, Skype didn't need to retain and pay for a billing department. Plus, the company did no advertising, which saved a lot in overhead costs. With this renegade business model, Friis and Zennström noted that the company would achieve financial success even if only 5 percent of its users paid for extras.

Skype wasn't without its competitors, though. In fact, it has many: traditional phone companies, cable and DSL providers, and VoIP providers such as Vonage are among them, though they all suffer from the same weakness of being expensive. Google Voice and Apple FaceTime are two major competitors, along with Facebook chat, GoToMeeting, and Cisco WebEx. Google Voice and Apple FaceTime are perhaps the biggest competitors because both technologies offer free services, including voice and video calls. However, FaceTime is limited to Apple users with a FaceTime-enabled device, which somewhat limits its market. And until recently, Google Voice was available only for PC users. Facebook's chat was originally limited to instant messaging, and both GoToMeeting and Cisco WebEx offered pay services, not free services. Skype, on the other hand, has featured both Windows and Mac support since 2006 and offers instant messaging, desktop sharing, and file-sharing capabilities, which FaceTime and Google Voice do not. Given this, it's no surprise that Skype has been the major success story in this technology.

The Impact of the Solution on Society

Friis and Zennström's business model took hold and paid off handsomely. In 2005, eBay purchased Skype for $2.6 billion. It later sold it to Microsoft in 2011 for $8.5 billion. The proceeds were divided among several investors, but Skype's founders reportedly got a cool $1.19 billion in the deal.

Today, many people around the world use Skype to communicate over long distances.

Why was Microsoft interested in communications service? Simply put, Microsoft could integrate Skype with its Xbox, Windows Phone, and various other devices and communities, such as Hotmail, Lync, Exchange Server, and Live Messenger. This was valuable to Microsoft given Skype's active client base of more than six hundred million users. More individuals using Skype meant more people also being exposed to Microsoft.

The popularity of Skype hasn't been kind to the phone company industry. Along with cell phone technology, Skype and VoIP technology have rendered traditional phone service nearly obsolete. Many people don't have landlines anymore, instead choosing to make and receive their calls through Skype or on their cell phones instead. However, the benefits to people have been numerous. Video calls have allowed people who rarely see each other to have virtual "face-to-face" conversations. Grandparents can see their grandkids with a simple call, rather than waiting for pictures to arrive in the mail or through e-mail. Likewise, in times of disaster, Skype has proven a much more reliable method of communication than traditional phone services. For example, after the Loma Prieta earthquake of 1989 in the San Francisco Bay Area, phone lines were quickly jammed, as people tried to reassure their loved ones that they were safe. Some people had to wait days to be able to make a phone call to find out whether a loved one was hurt! However, when a powerful earthquake hit New Zealand in 2011, people were able to quickly Skype their loved ones and let them know they were safe.

There's no doubt that Skype has changed the face of telecommunications. With more than six hundred million users, it is truly an invention that has affected many people, and the way they communicate, around the world.

Where Are They Now?

Since handing over the company to Microsoft, longtime business partners Janus Friis and Niklas Zennström have reportedly embarked on separate journeys, but both are pursuing interesting new endeavors. Before parting ways, Friis and Zennström also cofounded Altnet, a network selling commercial music; Joltid, a company that develops and sells peer-to-peer solutions to companies; Joost, an Internet TV service; and Rdio, an ad-free website for music streaming and downloading.

Friis has founded Vdio, a music and video streaming service, and Aether, a San Francisco–based company that has created a wireless music and audio player called the Cone. Zennström currently runs Atomico, an international investment firm based in London that focuses on tech companies that it feels are poised to transform the industry. He is also actively involved in Zennström Philanthropies, a charitable organization he founded with his wife, Catherine.

Timeline

1966
Niklas Zennström born in Sweden

1976
Janus Friis born in Denmark

1996
Friis and Zennström meet at Tele2

2001
Friis and Zennström launch KaZaA

2002
Friis and Zennström sell KaZaA after facing legal difficulties

2003
Friis and Zennström found Skype

2005
Skype purchased by eBay; Skype introduces video calling

2006
Number of Skype users reaches one hundred million

2007
Zennström forms Zennström Philanthropies

2009
eBay sells 70 percent of Skype to investors; Skype launches iPhone and Android apps

2011
Microsoft acquires Skype for $8.5 billion

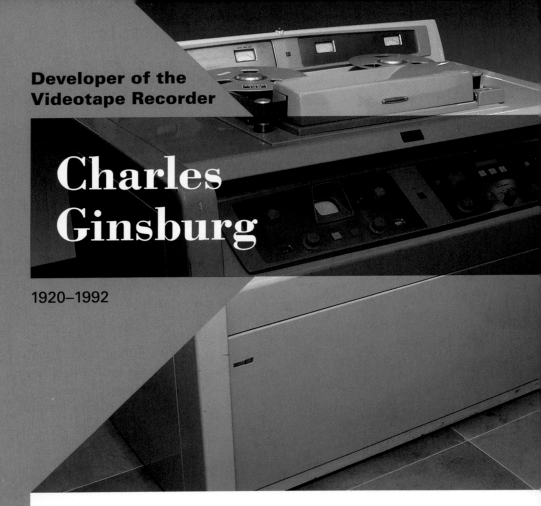

Developer of the Videotape Recorder

Charles Ginsburg

1920–1992

Starting in the 1950s, the world would see changes in technology like never before. One of the most significant advances in technology was made by a man named Charles Ginsburg and his team of development engineers. In 1957, they created the first working videotape recorder. This device would revolutionize the film and recording industries and would lead to the evolution of further video technologies.

An Inventor's Beginning

Charles Ginsburg was born in San Francisco, California, on July 27, 1920. When he was four years old, he was diagnosed with diabetes, a condition in which the body fails to produce the hormone insulin. Fortunately for Ginsburg, insulin had recently been made available to treat this potentially fatal disease, so he was able to keep his condition under control.

As a young man, Ginsburg was interested in science but was uncertain about what area he wanted to study. He entered the University of California–Berkeley as a premedical student, then transferred two years later to the University of California–Davis to study animal husbandry. Financial difficulties combined with an inability to focus prompted Ginsburg to drop out of college in 1940.

Charles Ginsburg

Ginsburg then worked at a variety of jobs, including as a sound technician for a San Francisco recording company in 1942. The next year Ginsburg worked as an engineer at a radio broadcasting company, a job he held until 1947. While working, Ginsburg returned to college to study engineering, earning a bachelor's degree from San Jose State University in 1948. A year before he graduated, Ginsburg switched jobs again, working as a transmitter engineer at a San Francisco radio station.

Defining the Problem

Ginsburg was eager to move into what was then the new field of television. He mentioned this to a neighbor who worked for Ampex Electric and Manufacturing Corp., a company in Redwood City, California. Ampex, founded in 1944 at the height of World War II, had been a military contractor, but with the end of the war it had moved into a new business: magnetic tape recordings.

Magnetic tape had been perfected for audio recording by German scientists during the war. After the war ended, American soldiers brought the technology back to the United States, where it caught on in the radio industry because it was cheaper and made recordings of higher quality than any other technology then available.

The popularity of magnetic tape in radio broadcasting suggested to Ampex's management that it might also be used in television. At that time, the lack of an inexpensive, high-quality method to record video was a major problem for television studios. Most shows were transmitted live—an approach that had serious drawbacks because any mistakes or inappropriate remarks were also immediately broadcast.

"The development of the first practical television videotape recorder did not flow from divine inspiration or a miraculous breakthrough onto the road to success. The first video recorder was the end product of over four years of hard, and at times, inspired work by a team of individuals."
—Charles Ginsburg

If a network wanted to record a show to televise later—for viewers living on the West Coast, for example—the show had to be filmed and the film quickly developed and then broadcast. This process was both difficult and very expensive—film is costly and cannot be reused. The need for videotape recordings was so apparent that Ampex was competing with a number of other, larger corporations, among them the giant Radio Corporation of America, to develop the technology.

Recording video, however, presented a serious problem. A video signal contained much more information than an audio signal, and no one knew how to fit all the information onto magnetic tape. Magnetic tape was made by coating thin plastic tape with iron oxide powder, which became permanently magnetized when exposed to a magnetic field. To make a recording, a recording head containing an electromagnet was passed over the tape. The strength of the magnetic field varied depending on what was being recorded, and the tape was affected by those variations. During playback, the variations in the tape's magnetism were translated into sounds or images.

In audio recordings, the information is recorded in one long, straight line running along the tape. When engineers first tried to make videotape, they also recorded the information in a long, straight line along the tape. However, because the video signal contained so much more information, recording a very short video clip required an enormous amount of tape; the length of tape that could record a half hour of music could record only a minute of video. Because the tape had to be so long, the video clip could be recorded or played only at such high speeds that, should the tape break, people could be seriously injured.

Ampex's head engineer, Walter Selsted, had seen what he thought might be a solution—an experimental videotape recorder with the recording and playing heads (the interface between the tape and the recorder) put on a small wheel that spun. The spinning heads permitted information to be recorded in countless small strips that ran across the tape rather than in one long strip along the tape. The tape did not have to be played at a high speed because the heads were themselves moving quickly.

Designing the Solution

Ampex's management decided to develop a videotape recorder with revolving heads. Ginsburg was recommended for the post of lead engineer for the program, and in January 1952, he went to work for Ampex.

Ampex, however, was working on several other projects at the time, and the videotape recorder was a fairly low priority. In May 1952, the program was suspended for three months to allow Ginsburg to help on a project to develop another recording technology.

While working on that project, Ginsburg met Ray Milton Dolby, a college freshman who worked part-time at Ampex. Dolby, who would later develop noise-reduction technology that

Ray Milton Dolby receives an award at the 2005 Technology and Engineering Emmy Awards.

carries his name, had heard about the videotape recorder project and was very excited about it. Ginsburg was impressed by Dolby's ability and enthusiasm. When the effort to build a videotape recorder was reinstituted in August, Dolby was made a part of the team.

Initial Troubles

In November 1952, Ginsburg and Dolby built a **prototype** videotape recorder. The quality of the recorded image was very poor, however, and Ampex's management was unimpressed.

The project received another blow in the spring of 1953, when Dolby, who had dropped out of school to work on the videotape recorder, was drafted into the US Army for the Korean War. It seemed unlikely that the project would ever be a success. In June, Ampex suspended the videotape recorder project once more.

However, Ginsburg continued to work on the project in secret. He was helped by another engineer, Charles Anderson, who joined Ampex in the spring of 1954. In August 1954, Ginsburg and Anderson made a presentation of an improved videotape recorder to Ampex's management. The quality of the images was much better, suggesting that perhaps the recorder could be successful. Ampex decided to restart the project once again.

Applying the Solution

The recorder was far from perfect. As the heads spun, they tended to create white lines across the video images. Ginsburg quickly went about assembling an engineering team to overcome this and other problems. The team included Anderson, Shelby Henderson, Fred Pfost, and Alex Maxey, and when Dolby returned from the army in January 1955, the team was complete. The six men threw themselves into work on the videotape recorder, developing new recording and playing heads, altering the design of the tape guide, and making many other improvements.

Ginsburg's team took a little over a year to perfect the video recorder, which was called the Mark IV. The device was made public in April 1956. The first television broadcast using videotape was made the following November.

The Impact of the Solution on Society

Ginsburg remained with Ampex until his retirement in 1986. Four years later, he was inducted into the National Inventors Hall of Fame. He moved to Eugene, Oregon, where he died in 1992 at the age of seventy-one. In 2005, he, Dolby, Maxey, Anderson, Pfost, and Henderson were awarded the first lifetime achievement technology and engineering Emmy Award by the National Television Academy for their contributions to the field.

Ginsburg's contribution was far-reaching. Videotape recording (VTR) gave television studios a practical means of recording shows; taped shows eventually surpassed live broadcasts in popularity. In addition, VTR made television broadcasts more professional, eliminating the mistakes and dead airtime that had previously plagued the industry. In the 1970s, videotape recording technology was miniaturized, creating the videocassette recorder (VCR), the first device ordinary consumers could use to record and watch video at home.

An Invention Revealed

By early 1956, Ampex's managers were so impressed by the quality of the video recordings Ginsburg produced that they decided to give a surprise demonstration of the recorder at a meeting in Chicago in mid-April. In attendance were more than two hundred managers of television stations affiliated with CBS Broadcasting.

The videotape recorder, called the Mark IV, was transported to Chicago without incident. The day before the meeting, however, the Mark IV was demonstrated to a CBS official, who complained that the image quality was not quite good enough. The engineers realized that they needed better-quality tape and made a last-minute phone call to the tape manufacturer, 3M Company, which flew out an experimental new videotape in time for the demonstration.

The demonstration was an enormous success and was met with cheers and applause. Ampex had expected to sell perhaps five of the Mark IVs, which cost $45,000; the company received orders for eighty-two machines by the end of the month.

Home video would threaten the entertainment industry by reducing the number of people who watched broadcast television, but it would also provide new opportunities to make money as ordinary individuals bought videos of their favorite shows and movies. The work of Ginsburg and his team eventually altered nearly every aspect of the television industry. By the twenty-first century, however, videotapes as the world knew them were almost obsolete, having been replaced by the compact disc and Blu-Ray. Still, the techniques behind videotape recording continue to this day.

Timeline

1920
Charles Ginsburg born in San Francisco, California

1948
Ginsburg earns a bachelor's in engineering from San Jose State University

1952
Ginsburg begins to develop his videotape recorder at Ampex

1956
Ginsburg's team unveils the Mark IV video recorder

1986
Ginsburg retires from Ampex

1992
Ginsburg dies

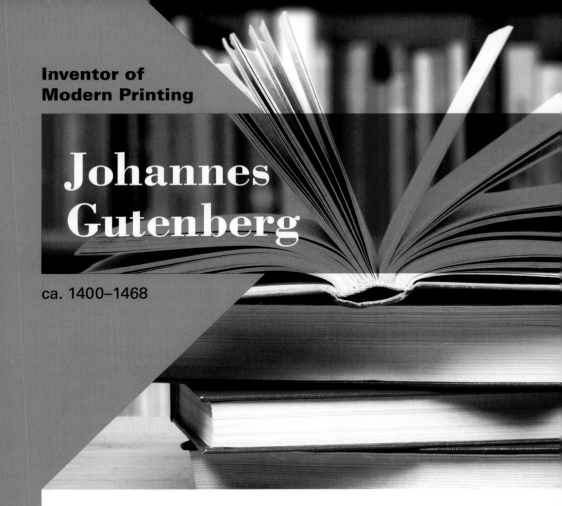

Johannes Gutenberg

ca. 1400–1468

F rom roughly the fourteenth century to the seventeenth century, Europe underwent a period of innovation called the Renaissance. It affected different parts of the world at different times, but over these centuries many noteworthy inventions were created. One of the most revolutionary inventions, arriving in the middle of the fifteenth century, was the printing press. Its inventor, a German named Johannes Gutenberg, would forever earn a place in history with his device. Before Gutenberg's invention arrived, books were copied out by hand or printed from hand-carved blocks. This took time; however, when the printing press arrived, it greatly reduced the pace at which books could be created and allowed more people to access books. Before long, the printing press had influenced changes in many parts of society—education, religion, science, politics, and business.

Mysterious Beginnings

Johannes Gutenberg made books accessible to people everywhere with his printing press.

Very little is known about Gutenberg's early life. Even his most famous years, when he developed the printing press, are shrouded in mystery. It is not even known exactly when he was born, though most historians agree that it was sometime between 1394 and 1400.

We do know that Johannes Gutenberg was born into a well-off family in Mainz, then one of Germany's most important cities and a major trading center. His father, Friele Gänsfleisch zur Laden zum Gutenberg, was a wealthy merchant; his mother, Else Wyrich, was the daughter of a shopkeeper. In those times, wealthy families had names that reflected where they lived: zur Laden zum Gutenberg showed that Friele Gänsfleisch had two separate houses in the neighborhoods of Laden and Gutenberg. Johannes was the youngest of three children.

It is not known where Gutenberg went to school, but given his wealthy family and the knowledge he would have needed to develop his invention, he probably had a good education. Clearly he learned to read and write, since these skills were central to printing books. Some historians think he went to one of the schools linked with the forty churches in Mainz. Others have suggested that he may have attended the nearby University of Erfurt because many wealthy young people were educated there, including some of his cousins. At some point, Gutenberg also learned metalworking, either from his father or from an uncle, but he would not have served an apprenticeship because he was an **aristocrat**. Although many jewelers and goldsmiths were based in Mainz at that time, the Gutenbergs played a special role: one branch of the family had long been responsible for the mint (making coins by stamping designs into metal). This knowledge may have inspired Gutenberg's method of printing.

Defining the Problem

Johannes Gutenberg lived at the end of the Middle Ages, the period of history that started around 400 CE, and the beginning of the Renaissance. At that time, few books were available and most people were illiterate; it is estimated that only one person in twenty could read or write in Germany at this time. Most of the books were large religious volumes such as Bibles, each of which had to be copied by hand from an earlier book. These books were called manuscripts (literally, "handwritten"); the "scribes" who produced them were extremely skillful but not necessarily that well educated (some could not themselves read or write). Some of the books they produced, known as illuminated manuscripts, were elaborately decorated with colorful inks and opulent designs in gold and silver. Each book took months or years to make and was very valuable, not least because it was unique.

Magical Mirrors

In the late 1430s, Gutenberg sold small mirrors (or "looking glasses") to the many people who attended a major exhibition of religious relics. Before people looked around the exhibition, they would pin a mirror to their hats in the hope that the mirror would catch some of the relics' magical properties and they could transfer these to their friends and relatives at home.

Printed books did exist in the Middle Ages, but mainly in Asia. The first printed book, known as the *Diamond Sutra*, was made in China in 868 CE. Each of the book's seven pages was carved from a separate flat block of wood, which was then covered with ink and pressed firmly onto paper so the carved design appeared in reverse. Once the block was made, it could be used to print a single page of a book over and over again. Sometimes very elaborate books were made with block printing. In the year 972, Chinese printers made the *Tripitaka*, a Buddhist sacred text. Each of its 130,000 pages was carved by hand from a separate wood block. Because carving small letters into wood accurately was difficult, block printing was most suitable for printing designs on picture cards, which were very popular at this time when so few people could read words. However, this type of block printing never became popular in Europe.

The big drawback of block printing was that many new blocks had to be prepared for each new book—a slow, time-consuming, and expensive process. The solution was to use not one large block to print a page but many smaller blocks to print each of the letters on that page. These blocks are called pieces of type; many different pages can be printed using the same type simply by rearranging the same letters to make different words. This invention, movable type, first appeared in China around the year 1000 and in Korea around 1300, but it was not a practical invention at that time. Asian languages use many thousands of picture symbols instead of our twenty-six letters, so a Chinese or Korean printer would still have needed thousands of tiny wooden blocks to print a book in this way.

Asia had developed a remarkable printing method but could not really use it efficiently; Europe had a growing need for books but no real way to produce them quickly. When Johannes Gutenberg "reinvented" movable type in Europe in the 1400s, he satisfied this need and caused a revolution. It is unlikely, though not impossible, that Gutenberg knew movable type had already been invented in Asia. Like many other inventions, it was an idea that was rediscovered and reinvented through years of painstaking experiments.

The First Book of Gutenberg

By 1430, Gutenberg had moved to the city of Strasbourg, where he seems to have tried a variety of jobs, including working as a police officer and a teacher (he taught a colleague, Andreas Dritzehn, to cut and polish gemstones). Around this time, Gutenberg also began to experiment with better ways of printing.

Although records are sketchy, historians do not think Gutenberg's invention was a Eureka moment—a brilliant stroke of genius that simply came to him in an instant. Like many modern inventors, he seems to have perfected his ideas by trial and error over many years, using several existing inventions together to make a completely new printing process. He began by printing from single, large, solid pieces of wood (block printing) and went on to experiment with printing using individual letters made from tiny pieces of metal (called type printing). He developed a way of moving those metal pieces of type to print many different pages, a technique called movable type. He also devised a new type of ink and a way to use a wine-making screw press to print pages evenly and reliably. With these innovations, modern printing was born.

By 1450, Gutenberg had returned to Mainz and was ready to start work on his first major book. This came to be known as the Gutenberg Bible, Mazarin Bible, or forty-two-line Bible (because each page contained exactly forty-two lines of words). It was a very ambitious

An engraving of Johannes Gutenberg's printing press

project. Historians believe around 180 copies were produced, each containing 1,282 pages bound into two separate volumes. Gutenberg clearly wanted to produce a book that was at least as impressive as a medieval Bible, so each copy was also illuminated and rubricated— marked with red headlines—by hand. The mammoth project seems to have been completed between 1453 and 1456. Gutenberg also worked on other publications at the same time, including a Turkish calendar that he printed in 1454.

Operating Gutenberg's Printing Press

Imagine Gutenberg's workshop—the heat of molten metal, the smell of wet ink, the rustle of thick paper, the regular squeak of the printing press. This humble place in the heart of Mainz was the birthplace of a new way of printing that changed human civilization perhaps more than any other invention in history. Gutenberg himself wrote, "A spring of truth shall flow from [my printing press] … Like a new star it shall scatter the darkness of ignorance, and cause a light heretofore unknown to shine amongst men."

Designing the Solution

Gutenberg did not invent printing, but in the course of twenty years of experimenting, he managed to improve every single stage of the printing process. He printed each page of his famous Bible using thousands of small pieces of metal type, one for each **character** on the page. Using small wooden wedges (called quoins), he arranged the pieces of type snugly in a wooden frame, or form, brushed the form with ink, and then pushed it firmly against a sheet of paper using a press. By covering the form with more ink and repeating the process, Gutenberg could make an exact copy of the same page. By rearranging the type to make new words and sentences, he could print different pages.

Before Gutenberg could print anything, he had to make his type. To make one letter, he used a sharp tool to engrave the shape of that letter into a piece of hard metal. This was called a punch because Gutenberg used it to punch the letter shape into a flat piece of copper called a matrix. Next, he placed the matrix into the bottom of a mold and filled it with hot **molten** metal. When this cooled, it turned solid and formed a piece of type. He used the same mold to cast many identical versions of the same letter; he used similar molds to cast all the other letters he needed. The words Gutenberg printed in this way looked more like handwriting than a modern book because he was trying to make printed books resemble old, handwritten Bibles.

The press Gutenberg used was a modified winepress. The ink-covered form, containing the type, rested on a wooden block; the paper was on top of the form; and another wooden block (called a platen) was moved on top of the paper. Gutenberg used an enormous screw on the top to tighten up this sandwich of materials and press the paper onto the inked type. The advantage of using a press was that it gave equal pressure across the page and produced an even print.

Gutenberg also made his own very thick printing ink. Carbon gave the ink its black color, and small amounts of metals such as copper and lead gave it a shiny quality. The ink was oil-based, not water-based, so it would stick to the metal type more easily. On some copies of his Bibles, Gutenberg also printed the red headlines called rubrics, but using two colors of ink proved slow and difficult, so this job was later done by hand.

Gutenberg did not, however, make his own paper; he used vellum or handmade paper imported from Italy. Gutenberg printed his famous Bible in a style called folio. He printed sheets of paper with two pages on each side and folded them down the middle to make one leaf. He collected around ten of these leaves to make a gathering, and he stitched about thirty gatherings together to make two volumes, each of about three hundred pages.

Applying the Solution

Like many other inventors, Gutenberg had to raise huge sums of money to finance his project. Constructing his printing equipment, particularly the many thousand letters of type that had to be cast out of metal, was very expensive. He managed to raise the needed funds by going into business with a wealthy moneylender, Johann Fust (ca. 1400–ca. 1466). Gutenberg had promised that they would see great profits from the business, but the three loans he took out from Fust, totaling around two thousand gulden (coins), were substantial—much more than an average worker at that time could earn in his entire life.

Gutenberg's downfall happened for a reason that is all too familiar in the history of invention. Fust was eager to see the profit from his investment, but Gutenberg was constantly trying to improve his idea and needed ever more money to do so. When Fust finally lost patience in 1455, he sued and forced Gutenberg to surrender his part of the firm. Without Gutenberg, Fust and his associate Peter Shäffer went on to publish a beautiful Psalter (book of psalms) in 1457, with two-color printing and two different sizes of type. Many people believe Gutenberg was responsible for these innovations.

Although Gutenberg was ruined, he managed to set up another printing firm and continued working in the Mainz area for several years. Historians disagree about his later life. Some say that he lived in poverty, but it seems he may have been more fortunate. In January 1465, he found favor with Adolph II, the archbishop of Mainz, who granted him a pension including a yearly allowance of grain, cloth, and 2,180 liters (2,304 quarts) of wine for his own use. He died in February 1468, about age seventy, and was buried at the Franziskus church in Mainz.

The Impact of the Solution on Society

The fifty years after Gutenberg developed his new printing method saw a huge increase in the number of printing presses in operation and books published. Books ceased to be one-of-a-kind works of art; suddenly, they were mass-produced items. Historians think that more than six thousand different titles were published during this time, including around forty thousand separate copies of the Bible. The technology spread rapidly through Europe, largely thanks to German printers who took their printing skills to other nations. The first North American printing press was established in Mexico City in 1539.

Gutenberg's development of movable type was the most important technological advance during the Renaissance. Books spread knowledge and allowed people to share ideas widely for the first time. Most of these early books were still published by the Roman Catholic Church, but people began to examine and discuss religious ideas much more closely and critically. Among those scrutinizing the Catholic Church and its theology were Martin Luther (1483–1546) and others; their criticisms of certain practices of the church and their alternative readings of sacred texts led to a huge period of religious upheaval known as the Reformation during which Protestant churches were established. Books helped to spread scientific ideas and knowledge, too, often pitting new scientific discoveries against the religious views of the day. By the 1600s, printing was also being used to produce newspapers and pamphlets, with an enormous effect on the spread of trade and political ideas around the world.

Printing advanced even further during the nineteenth-century Industrial Revolution, when the arrival of sturdy steam-driven presses made from iron allowed books and newspapers to be copied faster and in larger quantities than ever before. Hand-operated presses, such as Gutenberg's, could make no more than a few hundred copies per hour. By the 1870s, however, a roller press developed by American printer Richard March Hoe (1812–1886) was printing up to eighteen thousand newspapers in the same amount of time. Another great advance was the linotype machine, developed in 1884 by a German-born American printer, Ottmar Mergenthaler (1854–1899). It allowed printers to make up (or "set") a whole line of type automatically from molten metal, greatly accelerating the printing process. Printing using movable metal type continued until the 1970s and 1980s, more than five hundred years after Gutenberg, when electronic and photographic forms of copying and publishing gradually replaced it.

Although Gutenberg did not invent printing or moveable type, his improvements on already existing ideas greatly changed the way people interacted with each other and with the written word. It gave people new access to information, ideas, and texts that they had little concept of previously. In an age of invention, Gutenberg's printing press marked an important new era for technology and humanity. Its influence around the world can still be felt today, in modern-day printing techniques. There is little doubt that Gutenberg will continue to remain an important man in humanity's history.

Timeline

ca. 1400
Johannes Gutenberg born in Mainz, Germany

1430
Gutenberg moves to Strasbourg and begins to experiment with printing

1450
Gutenberg returns to Mainz

1453–1456
Gutenberg produces the Gutenberg Bible

1465
Gutenberg receives a yearly pension from the archbishop of Mainz

1468
Gutenberg dies

Narinder Kapany

1926–

Information in the twenty-first century is oftentimes communicated quickly and through multiple channels—the Internet, telephone, or television. For at least part of the journey, the way these devices carry information is through fiber-optic cables—hair-thin strands of glass and plastic that carry messages coded inside pulses of light. Fiber optics has been around a long time and owes its name and popularity to an Indian physicist named Narinder Kapany.

A Born Inventor

Narinder Singh Kapany was born in Moga, in the Punjab region of India, in 1926 and spent his childhood in the city of Dehra Dun. In school, he learned one of the most basic laws of physics: light

Narinder Kapany is known as the "father of fiber optics."

always travels in a straight line. Kapany doubted this immediately: "It became almost an obsession of mine to bend light around corners." The idea stayed with him when he went to the university in the city of Agra. There, he experimented with prisms, trying to bend light, but it always seemed to travel in a straight line.

Defining the Problem

Kapany, ambitious and eager to make his mark on the world, was determined to find a way to bend light. In 1951, the perfect opportunity arose. He had just completed his bachelor's of science degree at Agra University when an offer came to travel to London, England, to study for a higher degree in optics. He enrolled at the Imperial College of Science and Technology, where his supervisor was Harold Hopkins (1918–1994), then a young physicist. In 1954, Hopkins and Kapany were approached by some English surgeons who wanted to develop a flexible gastroscope that could be inserted down patients' throats to see inside the stomach. The gastroscopes then in use were rigid and painful to swallow. The problem seemed to involve making light bend around corners down a tube—but how would that be possible if light always traveled in straight lines?

Other Light Pioneers

Hopkins and Kapany were not the first to try to bend light. In the 1840s, Swiss professor Daniel Colladon found he could shine light down pipes filled with water. The light entered at one end and emerged at the other, even when the pipes bent around corners. Colladon realized that the water channeled the light in what he described as "one of the most beautiful, and most curious experiments that one can perform." Irish physicist John Tyndall achieved the same "light-pipe" effect in 1854. Today, Tyndall is widely known for discovering it, even though Colladon performed the same experiment and got the same effects a decade earlier.

Working Techniques of Fiber Optics

The fiber-optic cables used in telephone lines are made from one hundred or more optical fibers wrapped into a tight bundle. Each one of these fibers is a thin strand of glass or plastic that can carry millions of telephone calls or packets of Internet data at the speed of light. Lasers (powerful generators of pure light) send signals into one end of a fiber-optic cable, the signals travel down the cable to their destination, and light-detecting electronic circuits receive the signals at the other end.

Light signals travel through the cable by repeatedly bouncing off the glass walls. Although light can behave like a beam of rays, it can also be thought of as a steady stream of very energetic particles, known as photons. Imagine shining a flashlight into a glass rod so that photons of light pour into it. If the flashlight is held at an angle, the photons rush into the glass and travel in a straight line until they hit the edge of the tube. Then, just like rubber balls hitting a wall,

Light pipes were being used in theater sets and grand municipal fountains by the end of the nineteenth century, but many years passed before other uses were found. In the 1920s, Scottish television pioneer John Logie Baird and his US rivals C. Francis Jenkins and Clarence W. Hansell tried to use light pipes to transmit pictures. The following decade, German students Heinrich Lamm and Walter Gerlach tried to make a flexible light pipe that could be inserted into the throat to see inside the stomach. Although they had little success, they did manage to send a picture of the letter *V* down a very short piece of glass tubing.

Designing the Solution

In London in the 1950s, Hopkins and Kapany wrestled with the problem of making a more flexible instrument. They were soon developing extremely thin glass fibers, around one-third the diameter of a human hair, and using them to transmit images. With many thousands of these fibers fastened together, they made a thick light pipe and sent images of the letters *G-L-A-S* down it.

they bounce back at the opposite angle. They keep reverberating through the tube until they reach the other end.

The key to fiber optics is making the light stay inside the tube. Normally, if light is shone into the end of a glass tube, some of it leaks out of the edges, with the result that it does not normally travel very far down a glass rod. An optical fiber is specially designed to stop leakage. The central section of the fiber, known as the core, is surrounded by a different type of glass, known as the cladding. Although the cladding is clear glass, it is designed so that it helps to "mirror" the light rays traveling through the core by a process known as total internal reflection.

The initial attempts made by Kapany and Hopkins transmitted light poorly. However, in the words of South African physician Basil Hirschowitz, "It was flexible, and did transmit an image, and that was enough to set one dreaming."

Around the same time as Hopkins and Kapany, there were other scientists also thinking about bending light. Abraham van Heel (1899–1966), a physicist working at the University of Delft in the Netherlands, was using similar technology to make submarine periscopes. By 1952, he had also figured out how to send images through bundles of fibers. He explained his ideas in an article submitted to the scientific journal *Nature*; however, the article was delayed several months. It was finally published in January 1954. Hopkins and Kapany, meanwhile, had sent details of their own results to *Nature*, and these were published in the same issue. Although the English team had used a different approach, dispute arose about who had thought of the idea first. Kapany and Hopkins called their idea "fiber optics," and the name stuck.

The following year, at the age of twenty-eight, Narinder Kapany earned his doctorate and decided to leave England for the United States. He accepted a position at the University of Rochester, where some of the best research in optics was being done. Later, he moved to the Illinois Institute of Technology in Chicago, where he became head of the optics department. During this time, he wrote several dozen important scientific papers that established the basic ideas of sending light down glass fiber-optic tubes. This work earned him the name "the father of fiber optics."

Applying the Solution

Kapany's work was still mostly theoretical; some obstacles had to be overcome before fiber optics became a useful technology. When many thin glass fibers were fastened together to make a thick light pipe, the light that leaked out through the sides of one fiber into the others tended to spoil any image traveling through the pipe. In the mid-1950s, Abraham van Heel coated optical fibers with an outer layer of cladding. Cladding traps more light inside the core of the fiber, so the light travels farther without leaking out.

Three scientists at the University of Michigan—Lawrence Curtiss, Basil Hirschowitz, and Wilbur Peters—used van Heel's invention to make another breakthrough. They solved the problem of seeing inside the body when they invented the fiber-optic gastroscope. This instrument was a bundle of thin optical fibers wrapped together inside a thick outer sheath that a physician could push down a patient's throat. Light shone down some fibers from a lamp outside into the patient's stomach. Some of the light reflected back up other fibers into the physician's eyepiece, showing an image of the stomach. Curtiss later said, "This was phenomenal. This was one of the few times in my life when I knew that I had something that was truly going to be significant." The fiber-optic gastroscope was used for the first time in 1957 and was manufactured commercially in 1960. Other medical instruments—endoscopes, cables, and retractors—have since been invented. They use fiber optics to see inside the body, thus saving many lives.

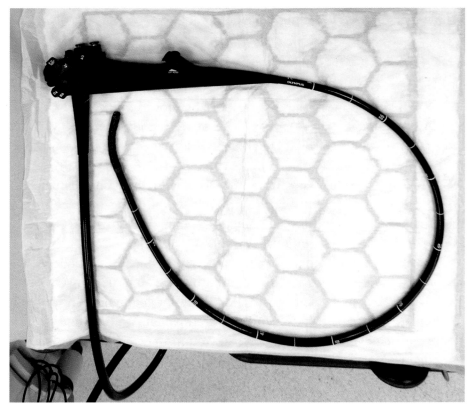

The gastroscope (pictured here) uses fiber optics to examine inside the human body.

Medical optics was an important use for the new technology, but many people dreamed of something more: sending information down glass fibers at the speed of light. Even with cladding, early optical fibers could not carry light very far. The light's energy would fade, or "attenuate," as the light rays bounced repeatedly down the fiber. This was fine for gastroscopes because they needed to carry light only a few feet or so, but it was not good for anything else.

A solution was devised in the mid-1960s by Chinese-born physicist Charles Kao (1933–), working in the United States at Standard Telecommunications Laboratories. Kao suggested that making fibers from very pure glass would allow beams of light to travel much farther. In 1970, a group of researchers at the Corning Glass Company achieved what Kao had described: a very thin, very pure optical fiber that could carry light signals long distances. Since then, fiber-optic cables have been widely used as telecommunications cables.

The Impact of the Solution on Society

Like many modern scientists, Narinder Kapany capitalized on his research by going into business. In 1960, he moved to the Bay Area of San Francisco and started Optics Technology, a company that made fiber-optic parts for surgical instruments. He stayed with the company for twelve years before starting his second business, Kaptron, in 1973. In 2000, he and his son Rajinder founded a third company, K2 Optronics, to develop advanced lasers for use with fiber-optic communication systems. In 2006, that company became part of EMCORE, a large fiber-optics organization.

For more than four decades, Kapany has balanced the roles of businessman and scientist, while continuing to patent new inventions and write books and scientific articles about the technology he helped to pioneer. Today, he has over one hundred patents on different inventions. His achievements have likewise won him awards, such as the Excellence Award 2000 from the US Pan-Asian American Chamber of Commerce and the Pravasi Bharatiya Samman of 2004, an award acknowledging noteworthy Indians who have excelled in their field. In 1967, he established the Sikh Foundation, which helps to promote Sikh culture in the United States.

Even though Narinder Kapany did not invent the fiber-optic gastroscope or telephone cable, he is known as the "father of fiber optics" because he was one of the key people who turned fiber optics from a science into a technology. Fiber optics began life as a nineteenth-century scientific discovery without a practical use. Following Kapany's work in the 1950s, people realized that this intriguing piece of science had practical uses, notably in medicine and telecommunications. Kapany was the scientist who helped to discover, name, and popularize the basic technology of fiber optics. Many others have built on his work, and today the industries based on fiber optics are worth many billions of dollars.

Timeline

1926
Narinder Kapany born in Punjab, India

1951
Kapany goes to London to study optics

1954
Kapany and his adviser coin the term "fiber optics"

1955
Kapany finishes doctorate and begins teaching at the University of Rochester

1960
Kapany moves to San Francisco and founds Optics Technology

1973
Kapany starts second business, Kaptron

2000
Kapany founds third company, K2 Optronics

2006
K2 Optronics becomes part of EMCORE

Hedy Lamarr

1913–2000

Inventors come in all shapes and sizes. Some even have completely different backgrounds than science and develop an interest in inventing through unconventional ways. Hedy Lamarr is one such person. A well-known actress in the 1930s and 1940s, she contributed to the development of radio communications during World War II. Her story is one of intrigue, and her invention was a lead contributor to other key communications technologies, including the cell phone.

The Inventor's Beginnings

Lamarr was born Hedwig Eva Maria Kiesler, on November 9, 1913. She grew up in an upper-class, well-to-do Jewish family in Vienna,

Austria. Her father was a bank director, and her mother a pianist. She was tutored from an early age, and she could play the piano, dance, sing, and speak four languages by the time she was a young teenager.

In 1930, the sixteen-year-old Kiesler enrolled in a drama school in Berlin, Germany, run by the famous director Max Reinhardt (1873–1943). That year, she made her debut in the German film *Geld auf der Strasse (Money on the Street)*. However, she is most famous for her role in the 1932 Czech film *Extase (Ecstasy)*, which featured her in the first nude scene in film history. She was just eighteen years old at the time, and the film brought her international fame.

Friedrich Mandl was an overpowering husband. Hedy Lamarr divorced him in 1937.

The film also brought her to the attention of Friedrich Mandl, a powerful Austrian arms manufacturer fifteen years her senior. The two married in 1933. Shortly after, Mandl put an end to his wife's budding acting career, and he kept her by his side as he met with and entertained some of the most powerful leaders in Europe, including Adolf Hitler and Benito Mussolini, as well as a host of arms dealers, manufacturers, and buyers. She listened closely and learned a great deal about the latest technology behind arms and munitions. Later, she would use this knowledge to invent a tool she hoped would destroy Nazism.

Hedy to Hollywood

In 1937, after four years of marriage, she left Mandl and fled to Paris, and then London. That same year, she and Mandl divorced. In London, she was discovered by the film mogul Louis B. Mayer. Mayer gave her a new name—Hedy Lamarr—and brought her to Hollywood.

Lamarr made her first English-language film, *Algiers*, in 1938 and quickly established herself as a powerful screen presence, though she

Hedy Lamarr was known not only for her intelligence and significance as an inventor but also for her beauty.

was celebrated more for her beauty than for her acting abilities. Over the next decades, she starred in more than a dozen films, including *Boom Town* (1940), *Ziegfeld Girl* (1941), *Tortilla Flat* (1942), and, in one of her most famous roles, *Samson and Delilah* (1949).

Defining the Problem

Lamarr's breakthrough as an inventor came just as she attained star status in Hollywood. At the time, war was raging in Europe. The Nazis had stormed through the Netherlands and Belgium and into France, and they were now threatening Great Britain. A fierce opponent of Nazism, Lamarr felt that she had to do something, and she had an idea.

"Any girl can be glamorous. All you have to do is stand still and look stupid."
—Hedy Lamarr

From her days entertaining arms manufacturers alongside her former husband, Lamarr was aware of certain difficulties with torpedoes. Without a guidance system, torpedoes were highly inaccurate. Radio-based guidance systems had their own problem—the radio frequencies were easily intercepted and jammed. She believed that rapidly hopping from frequency to frequency according to a predetermined synchronized pattern might permit torpedoes to avoid jamming or interception.

Designing the Solution

In 1940, Lamarr had become friends with George Antheil, a composer known for his elaborate, **avant-garde** musical scores. When she described her idea of "frequency hopping" to him, Antheil was intrigued, and he helped her with the technical details of the device. He believed that Lamarr's invention could be controlled in the same way that autopianos were controlled—with a paper roll dictating the changing radio frequencies. They spent months merging the crucial mechanisms behind radio transmission and player pianos. That December, Lamarr and Antheil sent a description of their device to the National Inventors Council (NIC). The head of the NIC saw the enormous potential of their invention and encouraged them to patent it.

After addressing some of the more difficult technical elements with the aid of an engineering professor, Lamar and Antheil applied for a patent for what they called a "Secret Communication System" on June 10, 1941. In the application, they described how identical paper rolls would be used to synchronize the frequencies in the radio transmitter and the receiver inside the torpedo. The patent called for eighty-eight frequencies—the number of keys on a piano.

The US Patent Office granted Lamarr and Antheil US Patent No. 2,292,387 on August 11, 1942. (Lamarr had been briefly married to screenwriter Gene Markey from 1939 to 1941, and she used the name Hedy Kiesler Markey on the patent application.) Shortly after, they turned their invention over to the US military. However, even though World War II continued, the military did not capitalize on Lamarr's idea. Some people say it was because the invention was too far ahead of its time; others suggest that the military was hesitant to put its efforts behind "flying player pianos."

Applying the Solution

Lamarr and Antheil's device languished, unused, for more than a decade. In 1957, engineers working for Sylvania Electronics "rediscovered" Lamarr's frequency-hopping concept and altered the technology to utilize electronic signals instead of paper rolls. Soon, the US Navy began to use frequency hopping—what it called "spread-spectrum"—technology to keep military communication channels secure. A type of spread-spectrum technology was used during the Cuban missile crisis in 1962. By then, however, Lamarr and Antheil's patent had expired.

About thirty-five years passed before Lamarr received credit for her contributions (Antheil died in 1959). In that time, spread-spectrum technology was introduced to the public and quickly transformed modern communications, opening the door for wireless (Wi-Fi) networks and cell phones. In 1997, Lamarr and Antheil received the Electronic Frontier Foundation Pioneer award for their work. The next year, Lamarr received the Viktor Kaplan Medal of the Austrian Association of Patent Holders and Inventors—the highest award given to inventors in her homeland.

The Impact of the Solution on Society

In the end, Lamarr earned no money from her patent and only much-belated recognition for her contribution to the field of military communications. In 1999, however, Wi-LAN, a Canadian wireless communications business, bought a 49 percent interest in Lamarr's original patent rights. Well into her eighties, she was finally being compensated for her work. Her response to the press was, "It's about time."

Sadly, this remarkable woman died alone in her home in Florida on January 19, 2000, at the age of eighty-five. In the days before her death, she was reportedly drawing up plans for new traffic lights—a testament to her hardworking, persevering nature. She will be remembered for her achievements in communications advancements and her influence on early film, and her legacy will not be forgotten.

Timeline

1913
Hedy Lamarr born Hedwig Eva Maria Kiesler in Vienna, Austria

1942
Lamarr is granted a patent for a "Secret Communication System"

1957
Engineers use Lamarr's concept to create spread-spectrum technology

1962
Spread-spectrum technology used during the Cuban missile crisis

1998
Lamarr receives the Viktor Kaplan Medal

1999
Wi-LAN pays Lamarr dividends from her original patent rights

2000
Lamarr dies

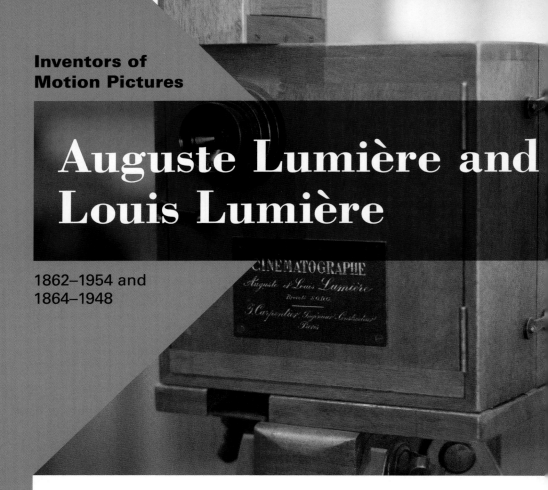

Auguste Lumière and Louis Lumière

1862–1954 and
1864–1948

Modern technology is often defined by advances in computer and communication technology. Film is one of the oldest modern technologies, arriving in the early 1800s. Films, or motion pictures, are visually engaging and still have the power to captivate audiences today. A movie lasting two hours is made from around two hundred thousand separate pictures shown in quick succession. In the 1820s, devices were created that presented a viewer with a stream of related images, and as the images rolled past, the person's eyes would interpret the pictures to be moving. By 1900, two French brothers, Auguste and Louis Lumière, had used this idea to develop the first practical movie-making equipment, produce the world's first movies, and open the first public movie theater. It was a discovery that would be expanded on and perfected through the decades but which would revolutionize humanity's entertainment industry.

The Brothers Lumière

Louis (*left*) and Auguste (*right*) Lumière in the 1920s

The Lumières were essentially scientists, but they owed their creativity to the influence of their unconventional and artistic father, Antoine Lumière (1840–1911). Although he began as a portrait painter, he was very interested in photography—a mixture of art and science that offered a quicker way of creating a likeness. Photography was still a new invention; it had been developed in France during the middle of the nineteenth century, when Antoine Lumière was a child. Antoine Lumière was enthralled with photography and could see that it would replace many types of painting in the future.

Antoine Lumière lived in the town of Besançon, in eastern France. He married Jeanne-Joséphine in 1859, and their two sons were born in the next few years—Auguste in 1862 and Louis in 1864. When France and Germany went to war in 1870, Lumière decided to move his family farther away from the French–German border, so they relocated about 150 miles (241 km) southwest, to the city of Lyon. There, Lumière opened a studio in a timber shack and made his living first as a portrait painter and later by taking photographs and selling supplies. He sent his young sons to La Martinière, the largest technical high school in the area. The two brothers showed considerable scientific promise, but Louis was a sickly child whose studies were often interrupted by crippling headaches, and he dropped out of school.

Louis Lumière quickly took up his father's interest in photography and, at the age of sixteen, began to experiment with photographic plates. These were pieces of glass, similar in size to those in a photograph frame, on which early cameras captured their pictures;

they were the forerunners of photographic film (a form of plastic coated with light-sensitive chemicals). The first plates were coated with wet chemicals and were slow and awkward to use. After much experimenting, Louis discovered he could make better photographic plates using dry chemicals.

Antoine Lumière realized how important his son's invention was and lent Louis the money to set up a factory where he could manufacture the plates. Over the next decade or so, the factory grew to become the biggest photographic supplier in Europe, employing three hundred people and producing more than fifteen million plates each year. The factory was a huge achievement and would bring wealth and security to the family, but it was barely completed when the Lumière brothers came up with an even more important invention that would take their lives in a new direction.

Defining the Problem

Their father had kept up his interest in photography and followed all the new developments. One of the biggest challenges was the effort to take photographs of moving objects. Early photographic plates needed a long exposure time: the iris of the camera (the part that lets light inside) had to be kept open for minutes or sometimes even hours to capture enough light to record an image. Thus only very still objects could be photographed, but many people wanted to photograph fast-moving objects and create "moving photographs" using a concept called the **persistence of vision**. When better plates (and eventually film) let people take photographs more quickly, the next step was to develop cameras that could swiftly take many pictures one after another and projectors that could "play back" those photographs later.

In 1861, an American named Coleman Sellers (1827–1907) devised a kinematoscope; he fastened a series of still photographs, each one showing a different aspect of a moving object, onto a paddle wheel. By shining a light on the wheel and spinning it, he projected the still pictures onto a screen and made them flicker into motion. The following decade, English-American photographer Eadweard

Muybridge (1830–1904) used a series of cameras arranged in a line to take photographic sequences of moving objects such as galloping horses and jumping gymnasts. In the 1880s, Frenchman Étienne-Jules Marey (1830–1904) made the first motion-picture camera. It had a mechanism inside that pulled photographic paper past a lens at high speed, recording a series of still photographs as it went. Unfortunately, it was not a very practical device: the paper was too weak and frequently buckled and tore.

Edison's Solution

Most of these inventors were working toward the same goal: to take many still pictures of moving objects very rapidly and then, somehow, to "play them back" later as moving pictures. That problem would finally be solved by the Lumière brothers, but not before another famous inventor, American Thomas Alva Edison (1847–1931), came up with his own solution.

In the early 1890s, Edison's assistant William Dickson (1860–1937) developed a crude movie camera called a kinetograph. Huge and cumbersome, it took forty-eight still photographs each second onto a reel of film punched with tiny "sprocket holes." An intricate mechanism inside the camera locked into these holes in the film and hauled it rapidly past the camera lens, while the iris blinked open and closed. Edison and Dickson, however, had no way of showing the films they took. Instead, they invented another device, the kineto-scope. People had to peer inside the kinetoscope to see kinetograph photographs, but only one person could look at a time. In 1894, Edison and Dickson opened their first kinetoscope parlor at 1155 Broadway in New York City, with others appearing in London, Berlin, and Paris the same year. Each parlor featured rows of coin-operated kinetoscopes showing simple movies of Wild West and circus shows.

When Edison's kinetoscope reached Paris, it caught the attention of Antoine Lumière, who had retired from the family's photographic business two years earlier. Greatly excited by the machine and the money Edison was making from the kinetoscope parlors, he went back to Lyon and told his sons, "You can do better."

Designing the Solution

The brothers recognized two drawbacks to Edison's work. First, the kinetograph (camera) was so bulky that it could be used only in an indoor studio, making outdoor movies impossible. Second, the Lumière brothers felt they should not have to peer inside a box to see the images. They promptly took up their father's challenge.

Auguste started work on the problem in the winter of 1894. Louis made the crucial breakthrough the following year, developing a claw mechanism that grabbed the film and pulled it through the camera. This innovation lay at the heart of their Cinématographe, an invention that combined movie camera, photograph printer, and projector in a single, compact box. On March 22, 1895, the Lumières organized their first movie screening for a private audience; on April 18, they patented the device; and they finally demonstrated the invention commercially nine months later on December 28. The following April, the brothers opened the world's first movie theater in a room at the Grand

Movie Theory

The key to making movies is to produce one moving picture from many still ones. In 1824, English scientist Peter Roget (1779–1869) discovered that if an individual looked at lots of slightly different still pictures, shown quickly one after another, his or her brain would be fooled into seeing a single moving picture. Roget called this idea the "persistence of vision." It happens because the eyes and the brain take time to process images.

In the early decades of the nineteenth century, inventors developed various toys with very unusual names that used the concept of the persistence of vision, including the zoetrope, praxinoscope, stroboscope, and phenakistoscope (also known as the phantasmascope and fantoscope). All worked in a broadly similar way; they had perhaps a dozen colorful drawings, each slightly different from the others, arranged on a large spinning disk or drum. As the disk or drum rotated, the drawings seemed to blur together to make a single moving image. Crude though they were, these devices were the world's very first animated cartoons.

Café in Paris. A combined movie camera and projector would have been of little interest or use without any movies to play, so they spent much time during 1895 making around sixty short motion pictures.

The movies they shot were very different from today's action-packed motion pictures. With names like *The Arrival of a Train*, *Feeding the Baby,* and *Workers Leaving the Lumière Factory*, they were simply brief (usually less than one minute) documentaries of ordinary things people did each day. Nevertheless, people in the audience were astonished by seeing giant moving images on the screen. A famous magician, Georges Méliès (1861–1938), vividly remembered going to the Lumières' first public movie show: "We sat with our mouths open, thunderstruck, speechless with amazement. At the end of the screening, all was madness, and everyone wanted to know how they might obtain the same results."

With such enthusiastic reactions, the Lumières realized that they could make a great deal of money from their invention. During 1897, they redesigned their photographic factory so it could manufacture and sell moviemaking equipment. The same year, they started to train their own film crews to produce even more movies for sale. Their catalog grew quickly; in 1897 they were offering just 357 titles, but by the following year they had produced more than 1,000.

Applying the Solution

The Lumières were not the only ones captivated by moviemaking; others could also see the huge moneymaking possibilities of their new invention. Edison promptly developed his own movie projector and, on April 23, 1896, showed the first public movies in the United States at Koster and Bial's Music Hall in New York City. The Lumières' Cinématographe reached the United States the same year. In France, Georges Méliès was so inspired by the Lumières' films that he began to make interesting and wildly imaginative movies of his own. Méliès was soon taking customers away from the Lumières; when he offered to buy their business, they declined to sell.

As the competition mounted over the next few years, the Lumières declared that, "The cinema is an invention without any future." In 1900, they sold the rights to their invention to Pathé, another film and production company; closed the moviemaking part of their factory; and turned their attention to other interests. Photography and movie-making had made them extremely wealthy, and earning money was no longer a concern for the Lumière brothers. Their father, Antoine, enjoyed spending the family's fortune, building several opulent mansions. Between 1899 and 1902, he built a luxurious residence, Villa Lumière, in Lyon, which was furnished and decorated by the city's finest artists and wood-carvers.

As the twentieth century began, the Lumière brothers were still young men with more than half their lives ahead of them. Like many other inventors, they continued to explore new ideas. In 1907, they invented the first practical color photography—a process known as autochrome. World War I (1914–1918) produced horrific casualties,

Breakthrough Invention

As the huge black-and-white locomotive thundered into the crowd, people suddenly panicked. Some screamed, some dived to one side, others shrank back fearing they would be crushed to death. What terrified the crowd was a fifty-second movie clip, *The Arrival of a Train at Ciotat Station*, made by Auguste and Louis Lumière. They had filmed the train moving diagonally across the screen—a clever artistic trick that made the train seem frighteningly real.

The Lumières understood that they could captivate the world with their Cinématographe. Auguste later wrote, "We had observed, my brother and I, how interesting it would be if we could project on a screen, and show before a whole gathering, animated scenes faithfully reproducing objects and people in movement."

The Cinématographe was made from wood and weighed just 12 pounds (5.4 kg). Essentially a movie camera, the Cinématographe not only recorded moving images but also developed movie film and played back recorded movies by projecting them onto a wall. To do each of these functions, it had to be used in a slightly different way.

Its first job was to take photographs, sixteen of them every second, onto a roll of photographic film stored inside the wooden and the Lumières devoted some of their energies to medical research. Auguste developed a gauze bandage used for treating burns, known as Tulle-gras Lumière, that is still used; Louis invented a mechanical hand that could be used by those who had lost hands in the conflict. Later, they explored three-dimensional photography using two cameras to take slightly different pictures, each of which was shown to a separate eye. The brothers continued to experiment and innovate until they died— Louis in 1948 at the age of eighty-four, and Auguste six years later.

The Impact of the Solution on Society

Movies and moviemaking technology developed rapidly during the early twentieth century because of innovators such as Georges Méliès, who produced the first "one-reelers" (longer films stored on spools); his fantastical *A Trip to the Moon* (1902) is still considered a classic.

box. To film a locomotive arriving, the operator would have opened the wooden box, loaded a reel of photographic film inside, and then closed the case. Having stood the camera on its tripod and pointed it at the locomotive, the operator turned a hand crank on the box at a steady speed. Inside the box, the crank drove an egg-shaped wheel, or cam, that moved two metal pins up and down. These locked into holes in the film reel, pulling it past the camera lens a little bit at a time. As the film chattered through, the camera lens flicked open and closed, taking one snapshot every $\frac{1}{16}$ second. The result was a series of still photographs on the film, each one recording a slightly different stage in the motion of the locomotive.

The Cinématographe could also be used "in reverse" as a projector. The operator opened the case and positioned a lamp behind it so light shone through the film. This carried the picture on the film out through the lens and made a much bigger image on the wall in front. Turning the crank threw one still picture after another onto the wall; turning it quickly enough made this series of still pictures merge together into a single moving image.

The Cinématographe made motion pictures popular. Today many people go to see movies in cinemas like this one.

Many silent black-and-white movies were produced in the United States from around 1910 onward by such producers as the New Yorker D. W. Griffith (1875–1948). More and more movie theaters were opened, many of them luxurious and reflecting the ever more glamorous nature of the movie business. By the 1920s, moviemaking had largely moved west to Hollywood.

Technology advanced, too. Silent movies gave way to movies with spoken dialogue and sound in the late 1920s, and the 1930s brought the first color movies (initially in just two colors). Although television and online streaming have had dramatic impacts on the movies since the 1950s, and people patronize movie theaters in smaller though still substantial numbers, movies continue to have a tremendous influence on modern life and culture.

The Lumières dropped out of the movie industry only five years after producing the Cinématographe, but their influence has lasted much longer. They invented not just the portable film camera and the idea of making films on location but the concept of going to the movies for entertainment. Their short films of everyday life led directly to documentaries and newsreels, but with their background in photography, they also brought an artistic and gently comic touch to their films that led to much more creative forms of moviemaking. Their invention ultimately made possible an entire culture of movies and a whole new way of looking at the world.

Timeline

1862
Auguste Lumière born in Besançon, France

1864
Louis Lumière born in Besançon, France

1870
The Lumière family relocates to Lyon, France

1894
Thomas Edison and William Dickson open kinetoscope parlors in New York City, London, Berlin, and Paris

1895
The Lumière brothers finish the Cinématographe and spend much of the year making short films

1896
The Lumière brothers open the world's first movie theater in Paris

1900
The Lumière brothers sell the rights to their invention to Pathé

1907
The Lumière brothers invent the autochrome process for color photography

1948
Louis Lumière dies

1954
Auguste Lumière dies

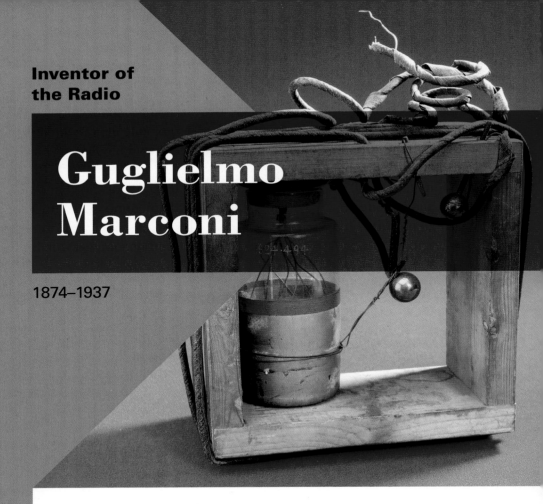

Guglielmo Marconi

1874–1937

When people think of a radio, they most likely picture a device used to listen to music in the car or inside their home. However, radios do more than just produce music. Radiotelegraphy—or radio, for short—is also known as "wireless" technology because it is a way of using electricity to send any kind of information between different locations without cables. Currently enjoying a rebirth in cellular phones and wireless Internet, radio was developed a little over a century ago by a young Italian named Guglielmo Marconi.

Guglielmo Marconi poses with the first radio devices, a transmitter (*left*) and receiver (*right*).

The Inventor Begins

Guglielmo Marconi was born on April 25, 1874, near Bologna, Italy, the second son of wealthy parents. His father, Giuseppe Marconi, was an Italian businessman; his mother, Annie Jameson, came from a wealthy family of Irish distillers (whiskey makers). Marconi was dismal at school and, although privately tutored, failed his university entrance exam. Nevertheless, he did take one course of lectures in electricity with an Italian physicist, Vincenzo Rosa, at Livorno, which made a lasting impression.

What Marconi lacked in schooling, he more than made up for with home study. He knew about James Clerk Maxwell (1831–1879), an Englishman who in 1873 had shown that electricity and magnetism are really two aspects of the same phenomenon: electromagnetism. Maxwell had proposed that electromagnetism could travel through the air in invisible waves at the speed of light, but he had not proved his proposition at the time of his death in 1879. Heinrich Hertz (1857–1894), a brilliant young German physicist, finally made some of Maxwell's electromagnetic waves (as they came to be known) around 1888, but he died six years later.

Defining the Problem

When news of Hertz's death reached Italy, Marconi, age twenty, read his obituary with interest and was struck by a new thought. Everyone knew messages could be transmitted by a cable using electricity—that was how Samuel Morse's electric telegraph had revolutionized communication in the 1840s. Hertz had shown that electricity could travel through the air. Marconi wondered if he could combine these two ideas to send telegraph messages through the air without using wires.

Designing the Solution

In 1895, he set out to find the answer. The young experimenter had already wired up the family's home, Villa Grifone, so he could flick a switch in one room and ring a bell in another using cables and electromagnets. Next came his experiments with wireless. Like any other form of communication, radio transmission involves sending a message from one place and receiving it elsewhere. Thus, two separate pieces of apparatus are needed—a transmitter to "throw" radio waves into the air and a receiver to "catch" them.

After successfully sending radio messages across his bedroom, Marconi took the apparatus outside to test it over greater distances. He found he could send messages farther by attaching high antennae to both the transmitter and the receiver and also by connecting both pieces of apparatus to the ground. He would send a message from the transmitter, and his brother Alphonso, standing some distance away, near the receiver, would raise a flag when he received it. Marconi was soon sending messages more than a mile (1.6 km). Flag signals no longer worked at that distance, so Alphonso had to fire a gun in the air instead.

Setting Sights on England

Marconi could see immediately that his invention was more useful than the telegraph because it needed no wires. His mother persuaded him to go to Rome, Italy's capital, to try to interest the government in his new invention. However, the Italian government had just invested a huge sum in a telegraph system and could see no reason for switching to something different.

This setback did not discourage the young Marconi; his mother knew many people in England, where much research into electricity was being done, and she sent him to London in 1896. According to one story, British customs officers tried to stop Marconi from bringing his strange bundle of electrical equipment into the country because they thought it was a bomb. Eventually he gained entry and soon met William Preece, the chief engineer of England's post office, who was enthusiastic about Marconi's ideas. With support from Preece and the British government, Marconi was soon carrying out bolder experiments and sending messages several miles.

"I would like to meet that young man who had the monumental audacity to attempt and succeed in jumping an electrical wave across the Atlantic."
—Thomas Alva Edison on Marconi

By 1896, he was so confident about his invention that he decided to apply for a British patent (number GB12039); he called his invention "improvements in transmitting electrical impulses and signals and in apparatus"—in other words, radio. During 1897, he formed his own corporation in London, the Marconi Wireless Telegraph Company, to sell the device.

Applying the Solution

Marconi had already shown that his invention could send messages over land, but communication at sea would really prove its worth. Telegraphs and telephones, which relied on wires, could not send messages to ships. Sea vessels still had to signal with semaphore (using flashlights or flags), which could send messages only as far as people could see. Radio proved an instant success for sending messages between ships and from ship to shore and back. Marconi's company quickly signed contracts with many shipping lines. In 1899, Marconi successfully transmitted radio messages 40 miles (64 km) across the English Channel, the narrow body of water that separates England from France. This impressive stunt proved that radio could be used to link entire countries. The same year, several British warships were fitted with radios, and Marconi demonstrated his invention to the US, French, German, and Italian navies.

Around this time, a problem with Marconi's system surfaced. Sending messages between one transmitter and one receiver was easy enough. However, if several people tried to send and receive messages at the same time, the signals would mix together. To solve this problem, Marconi came up with a radio that could be "tuned" to different signals. Instead of having every radio send and receive the same waves, Marconi figured out how different radios could be made to transmit signals using radio waves of different lengths. In 1900, Marconi took out a patent on this new innovation, which allowed radio sets to be tuned to different wavelengths.

Success followed success. In 1901, Marconi and his assistants carried out their boldest experiment of all. They sent a radio message across the Atlantic Ocean between Poldhu, Cornwall, in the southwest of England, and St. John's, Newfoundland, Canada—a distance of 2,099 miles (3,378 km). Because radio waves travel in straight lines, many people thought sending messages that far would be impossible—surely the waves would simply leave the earth's curved surface and fly off into space. Marconi's remarkable experiment showed that radio waves could travel between distant places on the earth. (Physicists later discovered that these transmissions were possible because the waves bounced off a part of the atmosphere,

Radio Science

Radio is a way of carrying information between two pieces of equipment—a transmitter and a receiver. The information rides on radio waves, which, like light and X-rays, are a type of electromagnetic radiation and travel at the speed of light. The radio waves that a transmitter produces have a certain wavelength. To pick them up, the receiver must also be tuned in to this wavelength.

Radio transmitters and receivers can take many different forms. The more powerful they are, the farther they can send and receive signals. An AM or FM radio station that broadcasts music programs uses a powerful transmitter and an antenna tens or hundreds of feet high to beam radio waves hundreds or thousands of miles. Cellular phones send and receive signals over shorter distances—typically just a few miles, to or from a nearby transmitter and receiver mast that connects them to the phone network—so they have smaller transmitters and their antennae are often small enough to be concealed inside the handset.

Most radio equipment still sends and receives information in what is known as analog form. That is, the up-and-down sound waves in a radio broadcast are carried through the air by radio waves, which also vibrate up and down. Increasingly, wireless technology is sending data digitally. Before information is beamed through the air, it is converted into a pattern of zeros and ones called binary digits. This digital information is transmitted to the receiver, which turns the binary digits back into normal information. Digital technology like this is used in cell phones, wireless Internet, and digital radio and television. Much more information can be sent in digital form (thus digital radio and television can offer many more channels). Digital information is also less subject to interference from atmospheric conditions.

called the ionosphere, like light reflecting back from a mirror.) Marconi's achievement was so astonishing that many refused to believe it had happened. Alexander Graham Bell, inventor of the telephone, said: "I doubt Marconi did that. It's an impossibility."

The Impact of the Solution on Society

Every year brought more success for the brilliant Italian. His wireless company made him wealthy. In 1909, he was granted the world's most prestigious science award, the Nobel Prize in Physics. That same year, the ship *Republic* collided with another vessel in the Atlantic Ocean; the crew used the ship's radio to call for help and virtually all on board were rescued. Three years later, the *Titanic* disaster was compounded partly because the nearest vessel, the *Californian*, had its radio switched off; 1,500 lost their lives.

In 1912, Marconi was caught up in a business scandal when the British prime minister, David Lloyd George, was accused of wrongfully trading in shares in Marconi's company. The same year, Marconi lost an eye in an automobile accident.

This misfortune did not stop Marconi from taking part in World War I (1914–1918), first in the Italian army, and later in the navy. In 1919, he was a delegate to the peace conference at Versailles, France, that formally ended the war. The Italian government soon made him a marchese (marquis) in recognition of his achievements. Marconi became very interested in politics, serving as scientific adviser to the Italian leader Benito Mussolini and becoming a senator in 1929. Being a senator automatically made him a member of Italy's Fascist Grand Council. Marconi was proud to support **fascism** even as its brutality began to unfold in the years leading up to World War II.

Whatever his other interests, radio was never far from Marconi's mind. During World War I, he had begun to experiment with radio waves of shorter lengths. Unlike the long waves Marconi had used until then, short waves could be broadcast with smaller and less sophisticated equipment. Marconi continued this work through the 1920s and 1930s. Around the same time, he developed a way of sending telephone calls with microwaves (very short–wavelength radio waves)—a technology now used in cell phones. The pope became one of the first to use this device, in 1932, when Marconi set up a link between the Vatican and Castel Gandolfo, the pope's summer palace.

Marconi died on July 20, 1937, age sixty-three, and was buried in a mausoleum at the family home. As a tribute, radio stations throughout the world fell silent for two minutes.

Controversy Claims Radio

When American inventor Lee De Forest (1873–1961) developed the audion (or triode) valve in 1906, the huge and cumbersome early radios suddenly became smaller and more affordable. The golden age of radio began with a broadcast from New York's Metropolitan Opera in 1910 and continued until the 1950s. Many people think television killed off radio at this time, but television was really just radio in a different guise; until the invention of satellite and cable, all televisions received pictures carried through the air by radio waves. Far from falling in popularity, wireless radio has become more important than ever, lying at the

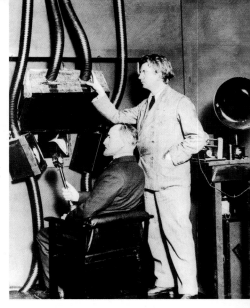

Scottish scientist John Logie Baird (*standing*) and Sir Oliver Lodge (*seated*) in 1926

heart of cellular phones and making possible one of the latest wireless technologies, Wi-Fi (Wireless Fidelity), a convenient way of connecting computers to the Internet without cables.

Just how much of the "wireless revolution" should be credited to Marconi is a matter of debate. He did not discover electromagnetism or radio waves, nor did he carry out the first radio experiments. England's Sir Oliver Lodge (1851–1940) sent a message by radio waves on August 14, 1894, several months before Marconi. Lodge also patented radio tuning in 1897, three years before Marconi. At first, Lodge accused Marconi of "inventing nothing and borrowing everything else," but he later sold his patent to the Italian and played down their rivalry. However, Lodge was not alone. A distinguished Russian scientist, Aleksandr Popov (1859–1906), also claimed to have made important discoveries about radio in 1895, prior to Marconi.

In the United States, Nikola Tesla (1856–1943), a Russian-born physicist, was granted the first patent on radio in 1900. As a result, when Marconi tried to patent his radio inventions, his applications were repeatedly refused. Then, in 1904, the US Patent Office reversed itself and awarded the patent for the radio to Marconi. This led to a long dispute between the two inventors until 1943 when, shortly after Tesla's death, the US Supreme Court overturned Marconi's patent and credited the invention to the Russian. This dispute demonstrates that great inventions are often the work of many people.

Marconi believed scientists who said radio waves could travel through the air. He went to great efforts to stretch this belief further and prove that radio signals could not only travel between short distances, but around the world. His invention may have been an improvement on already existing technologies, but the impact of his work has led to one of the most successful forms of communication the world has ever experienced.

Timeline

1874
Guglielmo Marconi born near Bologna, Italy

1895
Marconi begins his experiments with wireless

1897
Marconi forms Marconi Wireless Telegraph Company

1899
Marconi successfully transmits radio messages across English Channel

1900
Marconi patents device allowing radio sets to tune to different wavelengths

1901
Marconi sends a radio signal across the Atlantic Ocean

1920s–1930s
Marconi uses microwaves to make telephone calls

1937
Marconi dies

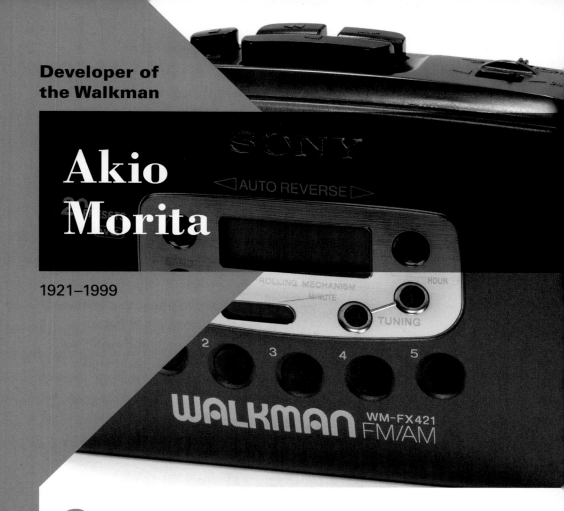

Developer of the Walkman

Akio Morita

1921–1999

One of the most celebrated inventions in modern times came from one of the founders of a long-standing technological company, Sony. Akio Morita was a well-respected businessman and marketer, but he would also prove he was an inventor. His creation of the Walkman portable stereo became one of the most successful advancements in music listening and a precursor to modern-day music players such as the MP3 player and the iPod.

Beginning Years

Akio Morita was born in Nagoya, Japan, in January 1921. His family had been in the business of brewing sake, a kind of rice wine, for about three hundred years. For the previous fourteen

Sony's founder Akio Morita

generations, the eldest son in the Morita family had taken leadership of the family sake business. Since Morita was the eldest son, his father prepared him from an early age to take over the business. However, Morita was fascinated by electronics, especially electronic sound equipment. He neglected his studies to build phonographs and other audio devices.

When the time came for him to go to secondary school, Morita decided that he wanted to attend the science program at the respected Eighth Higher School. His grades were not good enough to gain him admittance, however, so he spent a year being intensively tutored. He entered Eighth Higher School in 1937 and did well enough to be admitted to Osaka Imperial University, where he majored in physics.

Morita still expected to take over his family's business once his father retired, however. Morita's father was apparently more realistic; later he would say that he realized that his son's fascination with science would most likely take him away from the sake business.

The Second World War

During Morita's college years, Japan was engaged in World War II (1939–1945). At first, Morita's status as a student protected him from being drafted, but as the war wore on, Japan became more desperate for manpower. Morita saw that he would soon be forced into the military, most likely into combat duty.

In 1944, he found out about a program that permitted university students to continue their studies if they accepted a permanent position as an officer in the navy. Morita had no interest in a naval career, but any other option seemed likely to result in dangerous combat duty, so he joined the program.

He was able to complete his degree and was assigned to a group developing heat-seeking missiles. The group included Marasu Ibuka, who was thirteen years older than Morita and already had a reputation as a brilliant engineer. Morita was profoundly impressed by him. Ibuka's operation was moved to the countryside to protect it from US aerial bombings, and the two men lost touch.

After the United States dropped atomic bombs on Hiroshima and Nagasaki in August 1945, Morita wanted to be with his family, so he obtained permission to go home to Nagoya. It was there that he heard of Japan's surrender.

Rebuilding

For Morita, the end of the war was mainly a relief. No one in his family had been killed, and the family business had survived. The Japanese navy was disbanded by the American occupying forces, so Morita no longer had to worry about his commitment to be an officer.

Morita then received an invitation from a former professor to teach physics at the Tokyo Institute of Technology. While he was preparing for the move, he read a newspaper article noting that Ibuka was now in Tokyo and had started an electronics business in a bombed-out department store.

Once in Tokyo, Morita contacted Ibuka and offered his help. Morita eventually decided that he wanted to stop teaching and work with Ibuka full-time. He was wondering how to tell the school when he read that the Americans were going to purge former members of the Japanese military from teaching positions. Morita persuaded the Tokyo Institute to purge him early, and he left to work with Ibuka.

Sony Begins

In 1946, Morita and Ibuka first incorporated the company that would become Sony. Their firm's original name was Tokyo Tsushin Kogyo Kabushiki Kaisha, or Tokyo Telecommunications Engineering Company Limited. Although Morita's father was disappointed that his son was leaving the family business permanently, he invested money in the new company.

Ibuka had seen US troops with a tape recorder, then a new technology. He decided that the new company should make tape recorders, although neither man had any idea how to make one.

The partners eventually figured out how to build a recorder, but no plastic was available to make into magnetic recording tape. Morita finally obtained a supply of very strong, smooth paper, which he and Ibuka cut into thin strips by hand on the floor. They then brushed a magnetic coating onto the strips with soft brushes made from the belly hair of raccoons.

"I do not believe that any amount of market research could have told us that the Sony Walkman would be successful, not to say a sensational hit that would spawn many imitators. And yet this small item has literally changed the music-listening habits of millions of people."
—Akio Morita

Morita and Ibuka finally perfected their tape recorder, the first made in Japan. Most people who saw it thought it was a great toy, but far too expensive. Eventually, on the suggestion of an investor, Morita and Ibuka tried the Japanese courts, which were experiencing a shortage of stenographers. Morita later wrote, "They saw the value in the tape recorder immediately; to them it was no toy."

Selling the tape recorders was an eye-opener for Morita. He realized that marketing was essential to the company's survival. Ibuka was a very creative engineer, but he was not suited to managing a business. Morita, in contrast, had been immersed in the world of business from childhood, so he was the natural choice to run the business operations. From that point forward, he focused his efforts on determining what products would sell and how best to sell them.

Expansion of Sony

The company's next products centered on **transistors**, then a new technology, created at Bell Laboratories in the United States. Although many businesspeople were unsure if transistors would have commercial value, Ibuka and Morita realized that transistors could be

The Origins of Sony

During Morita's first trip abroad in 1953, he realized that his company's Japanese name was unpronounceable by foreigners and that the translated name was too long. He decided to create a new name, something short and easy to pronounce in any language.

Morita and Ibuka began consulting dictionaries and found the Latin word *sonus*, which means "sound." They liked *sonus* because they were making sound equipment and because it sounded like a slang term the Japanese had picked up from the Americans, "sonny boy," which meant a bright young man. They thought of using the word "sonny" but that sounded like a Japanese phrase meaning "to lose money." Finally it occurred to Morita to drop the second *n*, making the name Sony. The name was officially changed in 1958.

Naming the Walkman was more accidental. "Walkman" was chosen as the Japanese name because Sony already had a player called the Pressman on the market and "Walkman" suggested easy portability. Sony did not plan to use the name abroad, however, because it was grammatically incorrect, and the company assumed it would bother native English-speakers. The Walkman sold better than expected when it first went on sale in Japan, and Sony had to delay its introduction overseas by several months as it scrambled to meet domestic demand.

Reports began appearing in overseas newspapers about Sony's new Walkman product, and travelers to Japan started buying Walkmans and showing them to people back home. Morita himself traveled abroad frequently, and people in other countries kept asking him when the Walkman would be available. Finally, Morita decided that, ungrammatical or not, the name Walkman already had such recognition abroad that changing it would only cause confusion. The word now appears in most English dictionaries.

used to make electronic devices much smaller than those made with the technology they replaced, vacuum tubes.

Throughout the 1950s and 1960s, Sony released radios, televisions, and video cameras made with transistors. During those two decades,

Morita focused on developing a market for Sony products worldwide, particularly in the United States, where he lived in 1963 and 1964. At the time, products from Japan had a reputation for being cheap and shoddy. Morita decided early on that the Sony name should be associated with high-quality products that would sell at a premium. Accordingly, he guided the company toward more complex high-technology products rather than cheaper versions of existing products.

On the whole, the strategy worked. By 1969, Sony had sold a million of its portable color televisions worldwide. The company did experience failures, however. In 1975, Sony introduced the first portable videocassette player, the Betamax. Although a groundbreaking technology, the Betamax quickly lost out to another video player format—VHS (Vertical Helical Scan), which could play longer tapes. By the late 1970s, Betamax had clearly lost the contest. Because the well-publicized failure humiliated Sony, Morita wanted to develop a new product that would restore the company's luster.

In early 1979, Ibuka asked Sony's engineers to invent something that would allow him to listen to music when he traveled. The engineers took the Pressman, a portable tape player designed to be used by journalists, and attached a pair of large, earmuff-shaped headphones. The player had surprisingly good sound, but Ibuka found the unit too bulky and heavy. He showed it to Morita and shared his complaints.

Defining the Problem

Ibuka's player gave Morita an idea. He had noticed that young people, including his children, always wanted to have their music with them. At the time, that required carrying a radio or a tape player with speakers, forcing everyone in the area to listen to the music. If a lighter, smaller version of Ibuka's headphones-and-player combination could be created, then users could listen to better-quality sound wherever and whenever they wanted without annoying others.

Designing the Solution

Morita ordered Sony's engineers to remove the recorder and the speaker from the Pressman and to add small, lightweight headphones that the company already had under development. The product was designed as he asked, but Morita later noted, "Everybody gave me a hard time. It seemed as though nobody liked the idea." The concern was that no one would want to buy a tape player that could not be used to record sound. Even Ibuka, who had inspired this creation, doubted that the player would succeed.

Applying the Solution

In addition, Morita asked that the product be low-priced so that teenagers could afford to buy it. To make a profit, Sony would need to sell thirty thousand players, and no one expected that kind of sales volume. Morita finally offered to resign from his position as chairman of Sony if the player failed to sell thirty thousand units.

The Walkman went on sale in Japan in July 1979; all thirty thousand units were sold within two months. The device was a hit overseas as well. By the end of 1998, Sony alone had sold around 250 million Walkmans.

The Impact of the Solution on Society

Morita continued to lead Sony, and he created a high profile for himself internationally with his efforts to improve trade relations between the United States and Japan. A serious stroke in 1993 forced

Today, Sony is also known for its successful PlayStation consoles.

him to retire the next year. He remained under medical supervision until he died in 1999 at the age of seventy-eight.

Sony remains one of the world's foremost consumer electronics firms. Some of its most successful products in recent years have been the PlayStation, the Xperia Z cell phone, and the Xperia Z3 tablet. In 2014, the company had $69.2 billion in revenue. Sony is well respected in foreign markets, especially the United States.

The Walkman's success inspired other companies to populate the portable music device industry and bring entertainment to people around the world. For decades Sony and the Walkman were leaders in music-listening technology; however, that all changed when Apple introduced its iPod in 2001. Still, the Walkman's influence can be felt today. Many modern technologies—MP3 players, personal DVD players, and smartphones—owe their existence to Morita's portable entertainment device.

Timeline

1921
Akio Morita born in Nagoya, Japan

1946
Morita and Marasu Ibuka found an electronics company

1958
Morita and Ibuka's firm official changes its name to Sony

1969
Sony sells a million portable color televisions

1975
Sony releases the Betamax

1979
The Walkman goes on sale in Japan

1999
Morita dies

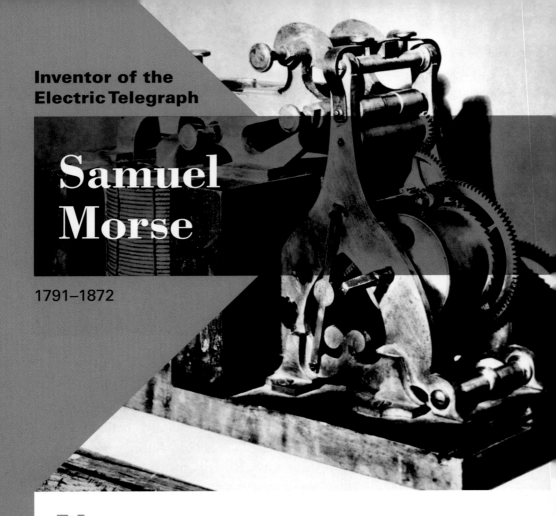

Samuel Morse

1791–1872

Not all inventors develop their interest for inventing at a young age, but many inventors end up changing the world in profound ways. Samuel Morse is one example. He invented the electric telegraph at age forty-four, and his device would transform the world in ways he could not have imagined. Eventually, his invention enabled the discovery of other inventions, such as the Internet.

Morse's Beginnings

Samuel Finley Breese Morse was born on April 27, 1791, in Charlestown, Massachusetts, now a suburb of Boston. He was the eldest son of Jedidiah Morse, a distinguished Congregational minister, and Elizabeth Ann Breese Morse. Although he was an erratic student at his school, Phillips Academy in Andover, he went on to Yale College (now Yale University). While there, he discovered he had a talent for painting portraits and dreamed of becoming an artist—to his parents' displeasure. When Morse graduated in 1810, he returned to Charlestown and worked as a clerk in a publishing firm.

Samuel Morse

However, Samuel Morse's artistic dreams refused to die. The following year, his parents gave in and paid for him to travel to London, England, to study art at the prestigious Royal Academy. During his four years in England, he learned what was called the "grand" or "historical" style, making huge, bold paintings of scenes from history and legend. At the same time, he met other young men who would also become famous, including the American artist Charles Bird King and the English poet Samuel Taylor Coleridge.

Morse's parents supported him through his studies, but when his money ran out in 1815 he returned to the United States. Few people were interested in buying huge historical paintings, so he was forced to make a living by painting portraits. Starting out, he found he had to travel between New England, South Carolina, and New York to make enough money with his portraiture. In 1818, he married Lucretia Pickering Walker in Concord, New Hampshire; their daughter Susan was born the following year.

Having a wife and family put a financial strain on Morse, and he tried to think of new ways to make money. One plan was to paint a huge picture of the House of Representatives, which he completed in 1822. He hoped to put it on display and charge the public to view it, but few were interested and the project lost money. Around the same time, Morse dabbled in his first two inventions: a fire-engine pump and a machine that could cut marble into statues.

These plans failed as well. Morse had now settled in New York City. He and his wife had a second child, Charles, in 1823, and Morse's standing as an artist continued to grow. In 1826, he and thirty other artists founded the National Academy of Design, with Morse as its first president. Six years later, he was appointed professor of painting and sculpture at what is now New York University.

Defining the Problem

While returning by steamship from a European painting trip in 1832, Morse passed the time chatting with a fellow passenger, Dr. Charles T. Jackson. Morse, who had long been interested in electricity, discussed with Jackson the latest scientific experiments that had proved that electricity and magnetism were two aspects of the same force. Shortly before, the Englishmen William Sturgeon (1783–1850) and Michael Faraday (1791–1867) and the American Joseph Henry (1797–1878) had made the first electromagnets (magnets that could be switched on and off by electricity). Henry had even suggested using electromagnets to send messages. As he discussed these ideas with Jackson, Morse grew excited and said, "I see no reason why intelligence may not be transmitted by electricity." For the rest of the voyage home, he sketched ideas for a device that could send messages down a wire.

Morse, an artist, not a scientist, had a limited knowledge of electricity. When he returned to New York, he began to experiment with electromagnets, building everything from scratch out of old clocks, painting easels, and other bits of junk. He could not even afford to buy the necessary insulated cable (metal wire with an outer coating to prevent signals from leaking away). Instead, he bought lengths of bare wire and wrapped it, inch by inch, with cotton thread.

By 1835, Morse had produced a crude working model of a telegraph. With this device, he managed to persuade a colleague, chemistry professor Leonard Gale (1800–1883), that the idea was a good one. Alfred Vail (1807–1859), a skillful mechanic, offered Morse help, funds, and access to his family's ironworks. By 1837, Morse, Gale, and Vail were partners in the exciting new project. Unknown to the Americans, two English scientists, Charles Wheatstone (1802–1875) and William Cooke (1806–1879), were already close to achieving the same goal.

Designing the Solution

The telegraph that Morse developed with help from Vail and Gale was based on a simple idea: electricity would travel along the length of a wire, and everything connected to it, making a complete loop called a circuit. To send a message down a wire, Morse realized he needed three pieces of apparatus: something to send the message, something to receive it, and something to link the sender and the receiver. The sender was a large switch (a "key") connected to one end of the wire.

Women's Role with the Telegraph

History remembers men as inventors of the telegraph and builders of telegraph lines. However, women played a prominent role in telegraph history—primarily as operators.

Operating a telegraph was a skilled job that involved sending and receiving messages in Morse code. It also required learning how to wire electrical equipment and keep it working. In the nineteenth century, women had few options for employment. Working as a telegraph operator offered women the opportunity to learn technical skills, do interesting work, and earn a decent living.

Many women worked in telegraph offices before getting married and having children or as a way to augment their husbands' incomes. Some raised children while they worked the telegraph keys, even moving telegraph keys into their homes, much like modern-day parents who use the Internet to telecommute while raising families. Although relatively few women rose beyond the rank of telegraph operator, some ran their own telegraph offices, usually in remote

When Morse pressed the key, it completed the circuit and electricity started to flow down the wire. At the other end of the wire was a recording device that used an electromagnet to cut a groove into a piece of paper each time a burst of electricity traveled down the wire. By pressing the key down quickly, Morse could transmit a brief electrical pulse along the wire, which made a short "dot" mark on the paper at the other end; pressing the key more slowly sent a longer pulse and made a bigger "dash" mark. Morse invented a special system, later known as Morse code, by which he could send the letters of the alphabet using different combinations of dots and dashes.

Cooke and Wheatstone's English telegraph worked differently, using a system of five wires and five moving needle pointers to indicate the letters that were sent. Because of Morse code and the dot-dash system, Morse's telegraph needed only one wire. Simpler and less expensive, it would soon make the Cooke telegraph obsolete.

outposts next to railroad stations. It was an important and responsible job, in which they also worked as signalers for the railroad, helping trains to run on time and ensuring their safety.

A woman uses Morse code to send a telegraph.

During 1837, Morse developed a working telegraph that could send messages at least 10 miles (16 km). He immediately applied for a patent. In the spring of 1838, he demonstrated the telegraph to influential congressmen, hoping to win their backing. In April of that year, Representative F.O.J. Smith of Maine asked Congress for $30,000 of government funds to help Morse construct a 50-mile (80-km) experimental telegraph line. That bill failed, and another five years went by before a similar bill was finally passed on March 3, 1843. This bill gave Morse the go-ahead to construct a 35-mile (56-km) test section of telegraph between Washington, DC, and Baltimore, Maryland.

Less than a month later, a team of workers began to construct an overhead telegraph line paralleling the Washington-to-Baltimore railroad tracks. While Morse stayed in Washington with a telegraph receiver, Vail traveled with the workers toward Baltimore, sending test messages down the line as each new section was completed. After several weeks, Morse and his partner sent the first official message by public telegraph on May 24, 1844: "What hath God wrought?" A week later, in a letter to his brother Sidney, Morse explained why he had chosen those biblical words: "It is his [God's] work, and he alone could have carried me thus far through all my trials and enabled me to triumph over the obstacles, physical and moral, which opposed me."

Applying the Solution

Few obstacles opposed Morse after that, and the telegraph spread quickly. Ten years after Morse sent his original message, 23,000 miles (37,015 km) of cable had been laid across the United States, mostly alongside railroad lines, which were expanding rapidly. In another decade, almost every city in the country was wired to the telegraph, and the Western Union Telegraph Company had become the country's biggest corporation. The next step was to connect different countries by laying cables under the oceans. Engineers eventually succeeded in 1858 when the first telegraph cable was laid under the Atlantic Ocean, linking America and Britain.

As the telegraph became increasingly popular, the new lines struggled to cope with demand. Better ways of using those lines were needed, and inventors worked intensively to develop them.

In 1872, J. B. Stearns invented a system (called duplex) that could send two messages down a telegraph wire, in opposite directions, at the same time. In 1874, Thomas Alva Edison (1847–1931) invented the quadruplex telegraph—it could send two messages in each direction at the same time (four messages traveling at once). He also invented an improved telegraph printer that could punch out messages very rapidly onto ticker tape. Even Alexander Graham Bell (1847–1922) tried to improve the telegraph, although his research led him in a different direction—to the telephone.

Envious of Morse's success, many inventors leaped on the bandwagon, and here Morse encountered a new obstacle. Some of these individuals tried to prove that they, not Morse, had been the original inventors of the telegraph. In 1837, Charles Jackson, the man with whom Morse had chatted on board the steamship, tried and failed to challenge Morse's new telegraph patent. The telegraph's success brought many legal battles, but in 1854 the US Supreme Court upheld Morse's claim to be the inventor and rightful patent holder.

Morse's Final Years

The legal challenges exhausted Morse, but he was rich and successful and his mind turned to other interests, including politics. Some of his views were controversial. He opposed the abolition of slavery, for example, because he believed the Bible accepted it. A passionate Nativist who opposed immigration, Morse ran unsuccessfully for mayor of New York City on the Nativist ticket in 1836 and 1841.

In 1847, he bought Locust Grove, an estate overlooking the Hudson River in Poughkeepsie, New York, and built a grand villa for his large family (which had grown to include seven children by 1857). He continued to be influential in politics and culture, funding many different organizations and causes, until his death on April 2, 1872, at the age of eighty-one.

The Impact of the Solution on Society

Many people marvel at how quickly the Internet has gained in popularity, but the Internet did not transform society as dramatically as did the telegraph 150 years earlier. Along with the railroads, the telegraph played a key role in the westward expansion of the United States, making the new territories easier to govern. Telegraphy revolutionized many other aspects of society because efficient long-distance communication enabled people to work together even if separated by great distances. Businesses set up a central headquarters that could communicate by wire to regional offices. Telegraph lines helped businesses to trade nationally as well as locally, and Edison's ticker-tape printer vastly increased the number of shares of stock traded, leading to the growth of Wall Street as the main national stock market. The press, too, underwent a revolution: news became easier to gather, so newspapers became more current and useful. The telegraph permitted information to flow back and forth across the country as never before.

While Morse did receive full recognition for the invention of the telegraph, other inventors helped as well. If he had not met Charles Jackson on board the steamship, he might have remained an artist and the telegraph may not have been what it became under his direction. Likewise, Alfred Vail and Leonard Gale helped make his device work. Above all, however, Morse could not have developed the tele-graph without first the invention of electromagnetism, the driving force of his machine.

Timeline

1791
Samuel Morse born in
Charlestown, Massachusetts

1810
Morse graduates from Yale College

1832
Morse discusses the idea of
a telegraph machine with
Charles Jackson

1835
Morse finishes a
telegraph prototype

1837
Morse applies for a patent for
the telegraph

1844
Morse sends the first message
by public telegraph

1847
Morse purchases an estate in
Poughkeepsie, New York

1854
The US Supreme Court declares
Morse to be the rightful holder of
the patent for the telegraph

1872
Morse dies

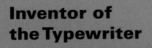

Inventor of the Typewriter

Christopher Latham Sholes

1819–1890

Many eras of history are recognized by the inventions or happenings that surround them. For example, the Renaissance is known as a period of renewed excitement, or "rebirth," of the arts and sciences; the Industrial Revolution was a period where factories and new mechanisms thrived. Similarly, today's era is often called the Information Age for its many technological advancements. Perhaps one of the first instances of the Information Age advancing into humanity occurred in the nineteenth century, when a man named Christopher Latham Sholes developed the first mechanical typewriter. It was an invention that would revolutionize communication as humanity knew it and contribute to other technologies such as the keyboard.

Pennsylvania Born

Christopher Latham Sholes was born February 14, 1819, on a farm near Mooresburg, Pennsylvania. After completing school, he went to work as a printer's apprentice. Several years later, in 1837, his family moved west to the then territory of Wisconsin. Sholes used his printing experience to enter the world of journalism. Over the next few decades, he edited a variety of newspapers in different parts of the state.

Christopher Latham Sholes invented the typewriter in Milwaukee, Wisconsin.

Journalism brings people into close contact with politics, an area that was of great interest to Sholes. After serving as the state printer for Wisconsin and editing the house journal of the state legislature, he served briefly as state senator. However, his health was unreliable and he lacked the robust personality needed for a political career. In his mid-forties, Sholes was appointed collector of customs taxes for the port of Milwaukee by President Abraham Lincoln. This less demanding job gave him more leisure, and he began to tinker with inventions.

Sholes had remained keenly interested in printing. In 1864, he and his friend Samuel Soulé invented a machine that could automatically print page numbers on sheets of paper. When another friend, Carlos Glidden, saw what they had done, he suggested to Sholes and Soulé that they modify their machine to also print letters. Glidden remembered seeing an article about a typing machine in the journal *Scientific American*. When Sholes read the article, he studied how the machine worked and decided he could invent something better.

Defining the Problem

Sholes was about to invent a mechanical writing machine, but he was not the first person to try. The idea of printing pages with small metal letters (known as pieces of type) was far from new. About four hundred years earlier, German printer Johannes Gutenberg (ca. 1400–1468) developed the modern printing press. Gutenberg's press used "movable type"—thousands of metal letters that could be rearranged in a large frame to print any number of different pages. Because arranging all the letters took so long, the printing press was better suited to making many copies of one page than to making one copy of a single page.

Inspired by Gutenberg's press, inventors tried to make a machine that could print single pages. In 1714, English inventor Henry Mill (ca. 1683–1771) was granted a patent for a "method for the impressing or transcribing of letters singly or progressively one after another, as in writing" that would make pages "so neat and exact as not to be distinguished from print." In 1808, Italian nobleman Pellegrino Turri built a machine so a blind countess friend of his could write letters. Louis Braille (1809–1852), the inventor of raised writing for the blind, also invented a typewriter for blind people in the mid-nineteenth century. American surveyor William Burt (1792–1858) was granted the first American patent for his Typographer machine in 1829. It had metal type letters mounted on a semicircular wheel. The operator turned the wheel to the right letter, pushed a lever, and the letter left its ink mark on the paper. Many similar machines appeared around this time. One of the most promising was invented by an American, Samuel Francis (1835–1886); with its black and white keys, it had the charming name Literary Piano.

Designing the Solution

In 1867, working with Soulé and Glidden, Sholes developed an enormous machine about the size of a kitchen table. The three men continued to tinker with their invention, and on June 23, 1868, they were granted a patent for their "Type-Writer."

Inventing is an expensive hobby, with money required to make endless prototypes. So Sholes used one of the machines to type a

The Workings of the Typewriter

With modern computer printers, entire books can be printed in just a few minutes. Everything took much longer in the age of the typewriter, when documents had to be produced laboriously, one letter at a time, using an intricate machine built of cogs, levers, wheels, and springs.

A mechanical typewriter has several main parts. At the back of the machine, paper is wrapped around a heavy rubber roller called a platen and held in place by a curved piece of metal or plastic. A piece of inked ribbon hangs just in front of the platen, feeding sideways from a spool on one side of the machine to a spool on the other side. The entire back part of the machine, including the platen, is called the carriage. It gradually moves the paper from right to left as letters are typed. At the front of the machine are rows of metal keys arranged in the familiar QWERTY layout. Each key is connected by levers and springs to a type-hammer that contains two small pieces of metal type—either an upper- and lowercase version of the same letter or numbers and characters.

When someone presses a key, it pushes its type-hammer up toward the paper. As it does so, the ribbon rises so that it comes between the hammer's metal type and the paper. When the type hits the ribbon, an inked impression of the letter presses onto the paper. When the key is released, a spring mechanism makes the key and the type-hammer fall back down. The ribbon spools turn slightly so a fresh piece of ribbon is ready to ink the next letter. The carriage moves one place to the left so the next letter does not type on top of the first. When a whole line has been typed, a bell rings to alert the typist. Pulling on a lever (called the carriage return) moves the entire carriage back to the right and turns the paper up slightly so it is ready to type the next line.

Christopher Latham Sholes

letter to a Wisconsin newspaperman named James Densmore (1820–1889), who had made money inventing an oil-transportation tanker some years before. Densmore immediately agreed to invest $600 in return for a quarter of the profits. Nevertheless, he was most unimpressed with the first clumsy typewriter prototypes and urged Sholes and his colleagues to try harder.

Before long, they had come up with a machine that enabled skilled operators to type words more quickly than they could write using a pen. However, levers connected the keys on the machine to small hammers that pressed the type-letters against the page. The faster someone typed, the more likely these levers were to jam together as they rose and fell in quick succession. In his earliest machines, Sholes had arranged the keyboard so the letters were in alphabetical order. Thus, letters that often occurred together (such as *D* and *E* in words ending in "ed") were near one another on the keyboard. When the keys were pressed quickly, their type levers tended to jam. Sholes solved the problem by rearranging commonly used letters so they were farther apart. That led him to the famous QWERTY layout (pronounced "kwerty," and named for the order of the keys in the top row of letters) that is still used in computer keyboards.

"Whatever I may have felt in the early days of the typewriter, it is obviously a blessing to mankind, and especially to womankind. I am glad I had something to do with it."
—Christopher Latham Sholes

The typewriter was improving all the time, but whenever Sholes made a new prototype, Densmore found fault and asked him to do better. Densmore kept advancing more money and buying an ever-larger stake in the invention. Eventually, he invested over $10,000 and bought out Soulé and Glidden, becoming Sholes's main partner. The following year, in 1873, the typewriting machine was as good as Sholes and Densmore could make it, and they managed to interest Remington & Sons, a gun-manufacturing company based in Ilion, New York, in producing the machine. The first Remington typewriters appeared in September of that year.

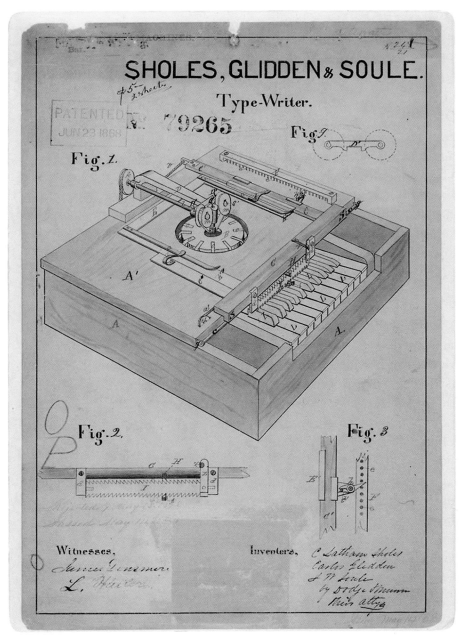

This is the patent drawing of the typewriter, illustrated in 1868.

Improvements

Early typewriters cost around $100 and were big and heavy. They also had a major drawback: they could print only in capital letters. Printing in both upper- and lowercase required two pieces of type for each letter. There were two solutions to this problem. One was to have two keys for each letter (thus entirely separate keys for *A* and *a*); some early typewriters had this format, which made them twice the size, much heavier, and more expensive. Then, in 1878, Sholes came up with the idea of adding an extra key, which he named "shift," to the keyboard so that both upper- and lowercase letters could be printed from the same type hammer. Punctuation marks and symbols were added above the top row of numbers.

Applying the Solution

The typewriter sold slowly in the 1870s but really took off a decade later. In 1888, a court stenographer from Salt Lake City, Frank E. McGurrin, invented a much faster way of using a typewriter. Known as "touch typing," it involved using more fingers to type and not looking at the keyboard so much. This helped to make typewriters more popular. As the machines themselves became faster and more reliable, they sold in ever-larger numbers—around one hundred thousand a year by 1900.

Christopher Sholes continued to tinker with his invention until his death in 1890. Despite the major part he had played in making the typewriter a success, he finally sold his remaining interest to James Densmore for only about $20,000. Densmore, the shrewder businessman, made an estimated $500,000 in the years that followed. When Sholes died in 1890, he was buried in an unmarked grave. In 1919, to observe the centenary of his birth, the National Shorthand Reporters Association erected a more fitting memorial in a cemetery in Milwaukee, Wisconsin. It read: "In grateful memory of the man whose genius has lightened labor and brought comfort and happiness to millions of toilers in the world's work."

The Impact of the Solution on Society

Dozens of people had tinkered with typewriters before Sholes; dozens more tried to cash in on the machine's success. The earliest typewriters printed on the back of the carriage, so it was impossible to see what was being typed without turning the paper over. "Visible" typewriters, which allowed the typist to see the letters being printed as they appeared, first went on sale in the 1880s. The rows of type keys used in early typewriters were replaced by type-wheels in some machines in the 1880s and 1890s. These wheels could be removed and swapped with different ones to change the typeface (font) being printed. The first successful portable typewriters appeared around 1910.

During the twentieth century, typewriters became increasingly automated after the first electric office typewriters appeared in the 1920s. In an electric typewriter, the keys are not directly connected to the type-hammers; instead, each key is a switch that operates the hammers electrically and the carriage moves back and forth electrically also. Electric typewriters are quicker and easier to use for long periods and produce a more even print quality. From the 1960s onward, electric typewriters called teletypes were widely used to enter data into computers and print out the results. They gradually evolved into modern computer keyboards, printers, and the word processing software that people use for writing today.

When Gutenberg developed the modern printing press, he put the power to spread knowledge into the hands of more people; when Christopher Latham Sholes invented the typewriter, that process went a step farther. Using a typewriter, one person could make professionally typed, single copies of letters, articles, and even books. A typewriter allowed anyone to set words in print and make them look important and credible.

Typewriters were also a huge force for social change. Along with telegraphs and telephones, they gave birth to the modern idea of the office: a place where information is collected and organized. Before typewriters were invented, relatively few women were working in offices. The first typing school for women was established at the New York Young Women's Christian Association (YWCA) in 1881—less than a decade after the first Remington typewriters went on sale. Within the next decade, around sixty thousand women were working as typists. For some, working at a typewriter in an office was not an improvement on working in the home. For others, typing skills offered a way to gain administrative skills and access to more ambitious business careers while earning their own income.

Some people think Sholes should not get credit for inventing the typewriter. After all, other similar inventions had been created before his. The typewriter he constructed with Soulé and Glidden, however, was the one that became popularized and adapted over the centuries—thanks to patronization by James Densmore. Without his backing, the typewriter as we know it might have ceased to exist. Today, typewriters are more often collector's items rather than pieces of equipment used in offices, though most present-day keyboards owe their layout to Sholes. Likewise, computer printers use some of Sholes's ideas. Sholes's innovative spirit paved the way for future communication technologies and transformed the way society interacted with the written word.

Timeline

1819
Christopher Latham Sholes born near Mooresburg, Pennsylvania

1864
Sholes and Samuel Soulé invent an automatic number-printing machine

1868
Sholes, Soulé, and Carlos Glidden granted a patent for a "Type-Writer"

1873
The first Remington typewriters appear on the market

1878
Sholes adds the shift key to the keyboard

1890
Sholes dies

Glossary

aristocrat A high-ranking member of society; a noble.

avant-garde Out of the norm; new, arty, or experimental.

camera obscura A darkened room with pinholes or slits poked in drapes over the windows to cast images onto an opposite wall.

character A letter, number, or punctuation mark.

codex An ancient book or manuscript, usually printed by hand.

commerce The exchange or buying and selling of large quantities of products and transporting them across large distances.

daguerreotype A photograph produced on a silver plate. The silver reacts with light, evaporating mercury in the silver, and an image is produced.

digital technology A type of computerized electronics that processes information in the form of numbers.

duchy Territory governed by a duke or duchess.

electromagnetism Magnetism developed by a current of electricity.

elocution How to speak words clearly.

fascism The violent political movement that brought to power Hitler in Germany and Mussolini in Italy.

IPO Initial public offering; a company's first sale of stock to the public.

molten Melted, as with hot liquid like lava.

optics The science of how light behaves.

packets Collections of related data that can be transmitted over a network.

patent A grant given by the government. It protects use of patented inventions in public.

Glossary

persistence of vision The theory that still images stay imprinted on the iris for a short time, giving the brain enough time to connect the image with the next one in the series, and so on, making the image seem to be moving.

physiology The study of the functions and activities of living matter (organs, tissues, or cells) and of the physical and chemical phenomena involved.

printing block A piece of wood on which letters are carved and that is used to print words onto pages of books; an early printing method.

prototype The first version of an invention.

radio A way of sending information through the air as a pattern of electricity and magnetism.

spread-spectrum communications A form of wireless communication that transmits different, varied frequencies across different channels.

transistor An electronic device that is used to increase or switch electronic signals and power.

vellum A high-quality, long-lasting material made from calfskin.

Further Information

Introduction to Communications Technology

Books   Briggs, Asa, and Peter Burke. *Social History of the Media: from Gutenberg to the Internet.* 3rd ed. Malden, MA: Polity Press, 2010.

DeGraf, Leonard. *Edison and the Rise of Innovation.* New York, NY: Sterling Publishing, 2013.

Poe, Marshall T. *A History of Communications: Media and Society from the Evolution of Speech to the Internet.* New York, NY: Cambridge University Press, 2011.

Websites   **Explore Invention at the Lemelson Center**
invention.smithsonian.org/home

National Inventors Hall of Fame
www.invent.org

Alexander Graham Bell: Inventor of the Telephone

Books   Coe, Lewis. *The Telephone and Its Several Inventors: A History.* Jefferson, NC: McFarland & Company, 2006.

Gray, Charlotte. *Reluctant Genius: Alexander Graham Bell and the Passion for Invention.* New York, NY: Arcade Publishing, 2011.

Meucci, Sandra. *Antonio and the Electric Scream: The Man Who Invented the Telephone.* Wellesley, MA: Branden Books, 2010.

Websites   **Alexander Graham Bell Speaks**
www.youtube.com/watch?v=4IJ6Pwb15JY

The Alexander Graham Bell Family Papers at the Library of Congress
memory.loc.gov/ammem/bellhtml/bellhome.html

Louis Braille: Inventor of the Braille Alphabet

Books   Frith, Margaret. *Who Was Louis Braille?* New York, NY: Grosset & Dunlop, 2014.

Further Information

Kent, Deborah. *What Is Braille? Overcoming Barriers.* New York, NY: Enslow, 2012.

Websites   **Braille Bug**
braillebug.afb.org

The Braille Institute
www.brailleinstitute.org

Louis Braille and the Braille Alphabet
www.youtube.com/watch?v=RYto5pSyy6g

Giovanni Caselli: Inventor of the Fax Machine

Books   Bly, Robert W., and Regina Anne Kelly. *The Encyclopedia of Business Letters, Faxes, and E-mails.* Franklin Lakes, NJ: Career Press, 2009.

Coopersmith, Jonathan. *Faxed: The Rise and Fall of the Fax Machine.* Baltimore, MD: Johns Hopkins University Press, 2015.

Naughton, John. *From Gutenberg to Zuckerberg: Disruptive Innovation in the Age of the Internet.* New York: Quercus, 2014.

Websites   **Giovanni Caselli**
www.britannica.com/EBchecked/topic/97867/Giovanni-Caselli

HowStuffWorks: How Fax Machines Work
electronics.howstuffworks.com/gadgets/fax/fax-machine2.htm

Martin Cooper: Developer of the Cell Phone

Books   Klemens, Guy. *The Cellphone: The History and Technology of the Gadget That Changed the World.* Jefferson, NC: McFarland Publishers, 2010.

Woyke, Elizabeth. *The Smartphone: Anatomy of an Industry.* New York: The New Press, 2014.

Websites	**How Cell Phones Work**
	www.youtube.com/watch?v=lJ9w3o5XTHc
	Tech History: The History of Cell Phones
	www.youtube.com/watch?v=fjJYw80OV1M

Janus Friis and Niklas Zennström: Cofounders of Skype

Books	Bjerge, Peder, and Lars Ole Løcke. *Billionaire on Skype.* Lystrup, Denmark: Scribilis, 2013.
	Courtney, Jim. *Experience Skype to the Max: The Essential Guide to the World's Leading Internet Communications Platform.* New York: Apress: 2015.
	Porterfield, Jason. *Niklas Zennström and Skype.* Internet Biographies. New York: Rosen Publishing Group, 2013.
Websites	**How to Use Skype**
	www.youtube.com/watch?v=sAIEWa_IEfl
	Zennström Philanthropies
	www.zennstrom.org

Charles Ginsburg: Developer of the Videotape Recorder

Books	Gomery, Douglas. *A History of Broadcasting in the United States.* Malden, MA: Wiley-Blackwell, 2008.
	Hilmes, Michele. *Only Connect: A Cultural History of Broadcasting in the United States.* 4th ed. Boston, MA: Cengage Learning, 2013.
Websites	**Charles Ginsburg Biography**
	www.anb.org/articles/20/20-01917.html
	Evolution of the Video Tape
	www.youtube.com/watch?v=uj32KXgorLQ

Johannes Gutenberg: Inventor of Modern Printing

Books	Kovarik, Bill. *Revolutions in Communication: Media History from Gutenberg to the Digital Age.* London, England: The Continuum International Publishing Group, 2011.

Further Information

Man, John. *The Gutenberg Revolution: How Printing Changed the Course of History.* London, England: Bantam, 2009.

Websites **British Library Digital Collection: Gutenberg**
www.bl.uk/treasures/gutenberg/homepage.html

Gutenberg Museum
www.gutenberg-museum.de

International Printing Museum
www.printmuseum.org

Narinder Kapany: Inventor of Fiber Optics

Books Ghatok, Ajoy, and K. Thyagarajan. *An Introduction to Fiber Optics.* Delhi, India: Foundation Books, 2007.

Hetch, Jeff. *City of Light: The Story of Fiber Optics.* Sloan Technology Series. New York, NY: Oxford University Press, 2004.

Kumar, Shiva. *Fiber Optics Communications: Fundamentals and Applications.* Chichester, England: Wiley, 2014.

Websites **America Revealed: Fiber Optics**
video.pbs.org/video/2229007191/

Optics for Kids
www.opticsforkids.com

Hedy Lamarr: Inventor of Radio Frequency–Hopping Technology

Books Rhodes, Richard. *Hedy's Folly: The Life and Breakthrough Inventions of Hedy Lamarr, the Most Beautiful Woman in the World.* New York: Vintage, 2012.

Shearer, Stephen Michael, and Robert Osborne. *Beautiful: The Life of Hedy Lamarr.* New York: St. Martin's Press, 2013.

Torrieri, Don. *Principles of Spread-Spectrum Communication Systems.* 2nd ed. New York, NY: Springer, 2011.

Websites **Official Hedy Lamarr Website**
www.hedylamarr.com

The Patent Files: Hedy Lamarr
www.youtube.com/watch?v=Nl8nOa9BvjY

Role Models in Science & Engineering Achievement
www.usasciencefestival.org/schoolprograms/2014-role-models-in-science-engineering/834-hedy.html

Auguste Lumière and Louis Lumière: Inventors of Motion Pictures

Books   Borden, Daniel, Floria Dujsens, Thomas Gilbert, and Adele Smith. *Film: A World History*. New York: Abrams, 2008.

Lavédrine, Bertrand, and Jean-Paul Gandolfo. *The Lumière Autochrome: History, Technology, and Preservation.* Los Angeles: Getty Conservation Institute, 2013.

Websites   **Arrival of a Train at La Ciotat**
www.youtube.com/watch?v=1dgLEDdFddk

How Stuff Works: How Movie Projectors Work
www.howstuffworks.com/movie-projector.htm

Institut Lumière
www.institut-lumiere.org/english/frames.html

Guglielmo Marconi: Inventor of the Radio

Books   Brodsky, Ira S. *The History of Wireless: How Creative Minds Produced Technology for the Masses.* St. Louis, MO: Telescope Books, 2008.

Kulling, Monica. *Making Contact!: Macroni Goes Wireless.* Great Ideas Series. Plattsburgh, NY: Tundra Books, 2013.

Townbridge, Calvin D., Jr. *Marconi: Father of Wireless, Grandfather of Radio, Great-Grandfather of the Cell Phone: The Story of the Race to Control Long-Distance Wireless.* Seattle, WA: BookSurge Publishing, 2010.

Websites   **Biography of Guglielmo Marconi**
videos.huffingtonpost.com/guglielmo-marconi-biography-119821429

Further Information

Nobel Prize—Guglielmo Marconi
nobelprize.org/physics/laureates/1909/marconi-bio.html

Akio Morita: Developer of the Walkman

Books   Atkinson, Sam (ed). *The Business Book: Big Ideas Simply Explained.* New York: Dorling Kindersley, 2014.

Gay, Paul du, and Stuart Hall, et al. *Doing Cultural Studies: The Story of the Walkman.* 2nd ed. Thousand Oaks, CA: SAGE Publications, 2013.

Websites   **Adventures in Tech: The Walkman's Amazing Origins**
www.youtube.com/watch?v=XBRmq3sYePM

Akio Morita: Entrepreneur Biography
www.entrepreneur.com/article/197676

Samuel Morse: Inventor of the Electric Telegraph

Books   Cassel, Melissa. *Who Was Samuel Morse?* West Conshoshocken, PA: Infinity Publishing, 2011.

Howe, Daniel Walker. *What Hath God Wrought: The Transformation of America, 1815–1848.* New York, NY: Oxford University Press, 2009.

Seidman, David. *Samuel Morse and the Telegraph.* Inventions and Discovery. Chicago, IL: Capstone, 2007.

Websites   **Museum of Obsolete Objects: Morse Code**
www.youtube.com/watch?v=L6gxfX4Grbl

Samuel Morse
www.samuelmorse.net

Christopher Latham Sholes: Inventor of the Typewriter

Books   Bie, Michael. *It Happened in Wisconsin.* It Happened series. Guilford, CT: Morris Book Publishing, 2007.

Weller, Charles Edward. *The Early History of the Typewriter.* London, England: Forgotten Books, 2012.

Wershler-Henry, Darren. *The Iron Whim: A Fragmented History of Typewriting.* Ithaca, NY: Cornell University Press, 2007.

Websites	**The Typewriter in the Twenty-first Century**
	www.youtube.com/watch?v=Z5XKQ8gZnXk
	Virtual Antique Typewriter Museum
	www.typewritermuseum.orgInde

Index

Index